WE PRAY

LIVING IN GOD'S PRESENCE

Oscar Lukefahr, C.M.

Liguori
Liguori, Missouri

Imprimi Potest: Thomas D. Picton, C.Ss.R.
Provincial, Denver Province • The Redemptorists

Imprimatur: Most Reverend Robert J. Hermann, V.G.
Auxiliary Bishop of St. Louis

Published by Liguori Publications • Liguori, Missouri
www.liguori.org

Library of Congress Cataloging-in-Publication Data

Lukefahr, Oscar.
    We pray : living in God's presence / Oscar Lukefahr, C.M. — 1st ed.
       p. cm.
    Includes bibliographical references.
    ISBN 978-0-7648-1561-4
1. Prayer—Catholic Church. I. Title.
    BV210.3. L85   2007
    248.3'2—dc22   2006039563

Liguori Publications, a nonprofit corporation, is an apostolate of the Redemptorists. To learn more about the Redemptorists, visit *Redemptorists.com*.

Printed in the United States of America
16 15 14 13 12 / 9 8 7 6 5
First edition

To Dean and Margo Bruschwein,
Ben and Kay Burford, Bob and Millie Fenton,
Steve and Patty Honnen,
Rob and Sallie Hurley, Hank and Jeanne Moreno,
Tom and Judy Morroni, Bill and Mary Rehm,
Chris and Anne Smith, Pat and Sheila Thorpe,
Brock and Kathy Whittenberger,
Bob and Mary Young—
For homes away from home (Matthew 19:29),
for prayer and friendship...Thanks!

OTHER BOOKS
BY FATHER LUKEFAHR

We Live
To Know, Love, and Serve God

We Pray
Living in God's Presence

The Search for Happiness
Four Levels of Emotional and Spiritual Growth

"We Believe…"
A Survey of the Catholic Church

Christ's Mother and Ours
A Catholic Guide to Mary

The Catechism Handbook

The Privilege of Being Catholic

A Catholic Guide to the Bible

CONTENTS

INTRODUCTION

~~❦~~

People enjoy the company of good friends, and prayer places us in the best of company: the Father, Son, and Holy Spirit! As the title of this book suggests and as the *Catechism of the Catholic Church* points out, "the life of prayer is the habit of being in the presence of...God" (2565).

We Pray: Living in God's Presence shows how prayer puts us in touch with God, how God speaks to us, and how we can respond. The book surveys what the Bible says about prayer, with an emphasis on the prayer and teaching of Jesus. It explains the many kinds and methods of prayer, and examines common questions and difficulties (for example, "Why isn't my prayer answered?" "Why do Catholics pray to the saints?"). Finally, the book shows how prayer directs us to heaven, the perfection of prayer, and the happiness of God's presence forever.

A life of prayer is possible only with God's help. Where do we find God? God is everywhere, and as Saint Paul states, in God "we live and move and have our being" (Acts 17:28). Yet we instinctively look up to heaven when we pray. In this we imitate Jesus, who at the Last Supper, "looked up to heaven and said, 'Father, the hour has come; glorify your Son so that the Son may glorify you'" (John 17:1).

We raise our eyes to heaven to seek the guidance of the Holy Spirit, who "helps us in our weakness; for we do not know how to pray as we ought, but that very Spirit intercedes with sighs too deep for words" (Romans 8:26). Here again, Jesus is our model, for after he was baptized by John "and was praying, the heaven was opened, and the Holy Spirit descended upon him in bodily form like a dove" (Luke 3:21-22).

That's why the cover directs our gaze to heaven, where we see the Holy Spirit as a dove. The staircase suggests that the path of prayer is not direct, but one that spirals upward. At times life takes us into the bright light of joy, at other times into the shadows of sorrow. But if we continue to lift up our eyes to the Father, knowing that we travel with Jesus at our side, certain that the Holy Spirit will help us in our weakness, we will discover that the life of prayer is indeed "living in God's presence."

My prayer is that you will be blessed by this book and by the teachings of the Bible and the *Catechism* on which it relies. I pray that its use of stories, humor, and events from the everyday lives of real people will show how prayer can be a joyful experience that leads us to the happiness of heaven.

My thanks to all who helped in the writing of *We Pray: Living in God's Presence*...to editor Danny Michaels, who suggested this project and whose advice, enthusiasm, and assistance were invaluable; to production editor Cecelia Portlock; to Judy Ahlers, copyeditor; to Evelyn John, formatting and layout; to Jodi Hendrickson, cover art and design, and to all at Liguori Publications who helped with this project. Thanks to Paul and Carol Berens, Mike and Mary Etta Dunaway, Frank and Gail Jones, and Den and Kathy Vollink, who discussed each chapter at our monthly study group meetings; special thanks to Carol Berens, who proofread the original manuscript and made many excellent suggestions. Thanks to the religious education class of Saint Vincent de Paul Parish in Perryville, Missouri, and to Sister Delores Schilli. Thanks to Rob and Sallie Hurley, Pat and Sheila Thorpe, Hank and Jeanne Moreno, Bill and Mary Rehm, Jerry and Susie Buckley, Betty Essner, Sheila Ortega, and Cathy Selby for ideas and encouragement. May God bless you all!

FATHER OSCAR LUKEFAHR, C.M.

Chapter One

DID YOU HEAR
WHAT GOD SAID?

A newspaper reporter covering the Jewish-Arab conflict in Israel decided to look for human-interest stories. She heard about an old man in Jerusalem who had been going to pray at the Wailing Wall for a long time. She went to the Wall and found him there. "Sir," she asked, "how long have you been coming to the Wailing Wall?" "I've been coming here every day for fifty years," he replied. "What do you pray for?" she inquired. "I pray for peace between Jews and Arabs. I pray that our children will grow up in friendship and harmony." "That's wonderful," she said. "How do you feel after praying here at the Wailing Wall for fifty years?" "I feel," he said, "like I've been talking to a wall."

When we ask God for specific things and don't get what we want, it may seem like we are talking to a wall. But prayer is more than asking. Prayer is communicating with God. The *Catechism of the Catholic Church* states that "the life of prayer is the habit of being in the presence of...God and in communion with him" (2565).

Being in communion with someone means that there is two-way communication. God has been around forever. God thought of us long before we were born. And prayer doesn't begin with us. God has already started the conversation by speaking to us.

HOW DOES GOD SPEAK?

Reggie White, the great National Football League defensive lineman, was also an ordained minister. When he became a free agent in 1993, he said he would wait for God to tell him where to play. He ended up signing a four-year $17 million contract with the Green Bay Packers. Later, Packers Coach Mike Holmgren admitted that he'd left a message on White's answering machine: "Reggie, this is God. Go to Green Bay."

God doesn't leave messages on answering machines! How does God speak to us? A comparison with human communication might be helpful.

Chris and Suzanne are expecting their first child. By giving their child life, they are calling her into a life of union with them.

By creating us, God calls us to a life of union with him. What God said to Jeremiah he says to us, "Before I formed you in the womb I knew you" (1:5). God gives life to each of us and so invites us to a life of communion. Conversation with God begins at the moment of conception.

Suzanne embraces the child with her whole being. Chris places his hand over the child and feels the baby move.

God embraces us with tender love, as a mother embraces her unborn child with her body. In God, "we live and move and have our being" (Acts 17:28). This embrace of God begins at conception, and it is God's will that the embrace should never end.

After their daughter is born, Suzanne and Chris hold Jessica close, feed her, clothe her, and encourage her as she takes her first steps.

God speaks to us through the events in our lives, by providential care:

I led them with cords of human kindness,
with bands of love.
I was to them like those
who lift infants to their cheeks.
I bent down to them and fed them" (Hosea 11:4).

The LORD *is my shepherd....*
He leads me in right paths
*   for his name's sake* (Psalm 23:1, 3).

Chris and Suzanne communicate love to Jessica with hugs
and kisses, with gifts and keepsakes she will treasure her whole
life long.

God communicates love through the created universe. In every good and beautiful thing we hear the voice of God:

The heavens are telling the glory of God;
*   and the firmament proclaims his handiwork.*
Day to day pours forth speech,
*   and night to night declares knowledge...*
their voice goes out through all the earth,
*   and their words to the end of the world* (Psalm 19:1–2, 4).

God showers gifts without number upon us. Scripture proclaims that God knows even better than parents how to bestow the best of gifts: "If you...know how to give good gifts to your children, how much more will your Father in heaven give good things to those who ask him!" (Matthew 7:11).

Of all God's gifts of love, the greatest is Jesus: "For God so loved the world that he gave his only Son, so that everyone who believes in him may not perish but may have eternal life" (John 3:16). And Jesus gave his very life for us: "No one has greater love than this, to lay down one's life for one's friends" (John 15:13). The gift continues until the end of time in the Eucharist: "This is my body, which is given for you" (Luke 22:19).

Chris and Suzanne speak words of love and invite Jessica to respond. They read stories to teach and entertain.

God speaks to us through the Bible, which is "living and active, sharper than any two-edged sword, piercing until it divides soul from spirit, joints from marrow; it is able to judge the thoughts and intentions of the heart" (Hebrews 4:12). God speaks to us through the prophets (Matthew 1:22; Acts 3:18). Above all, God speaks to us through Jesus (Hebrews 1:1–2). Jesus is "the Word" of God: "In the beginning was the Word, and the Word was with God, and the Word was God....And the Word became flesh" (John 1:1, 14).

As Jessica matures, communication between child and parents develops and is enriched. At times, parents and child enjoy just being in one another's presence, as their love finds expression in silence.

God also can address us in times of silence when we are quietly attentive to the Divine Presence (divine means "of or pertaining to" God). God evokes memories, stirs emotions, stimulates ideas and images, and encourages us to act. God can speak to us in the memories, feelings, thoughts, images, and decisions that arise in us. When they are of God, they will be in accord with the teachings of Scripture and the Church and will produce the good fruits of love, service, generosity, and peace.

HEAVENLY MESSENGERS

Brother David, principal of a Catholic high school in southeast Missouri, tells of an adventure he had in first grade. On the day before the feast of the Annunciation, the nun teaching his class told the children to ask their mothers this question: "What would you say if an angel appeared to you and invited you to be the mother of God?" His family lived in a neighborhood of varied races and nationalities. David skipped past their homes, including the house of their next-door neighbors, a Jewish couple,

Abe and Shirley Abrahamson. He could hardly wait to ask his mother the question. When he arrived home, his mother was in the kitchen, frying veal cutlets for supper. He eagerly asked what she would say if an angel invited her to be the mother of God. Without batting an eye, and continuing to flip the veal cutlets, she replied, "I would say: 'Wrong house. You want the Jewish girl next door.'"

It's a good thing Mary didn't answer the angel with those words! God does speak to people through heavenly messengers. Angels are immortal spiritual beings created by God with intelligence and free will. The word *angel* means "messenger," and angels are mentioned throughout Scripture as those who watch over people and deliver God's word to them (CCC 325–336).

The angel Gabriel, for example, announced the birth of John the Baptist to Zechariah, and told Mary of God's wish that she be the Mother of Jesus (Luke 1). Angels appeared to Joseph, to the shepherds at Christ's birth, and to many others before and after Christ's resurrection (Matthew 1–2; 28). Angels ministered to Jesus in the desert (Matthew 4:11), and an angel strengthened him in the Garden of Gethsemane (Luke 22:43).

Human beings who have died and are in God's presence may also relay God's word to us. Jesus himself spoke with heavenly visitors. When he was journeying to Jerusalem on the way to his crucifixion, Moses and Elijah visited with him on the Mount of Transfiguration (Luke 9:28–31). After Jesus' resurrection, saints rose from their graves and appeared to people on earth, no doubt to announce the good news that Jesus had risen (Matthew 27:52–53).

Countless people have reported visions or angels and saints. Dr. Diane Komp, a specialist in pediatric oncology at Yale University, records a number of such experiences in her book, *Images of Grace*. Dr. Komp was so convinced of the reality of these events that she moved from atheism to a firm belief in Jesus Christ as Savior.

The Church is cautious in its approach to miraculous appearances. People can be deceived by their own imaginations or emotions, or by the devil. Paul explains, "Even Satan disguises himself as an angel of light" (2 Corinthians 11:14). But the Church acknowledges that appearances and visions do happen and that some are worthy of belief, as shown in its approval of Mary's appearances at Lourdes, Fátima, and elsewhere.

And, of course, we don't need miracles for communication with angels and saints. Those in heaven know what is happening on earth. Jesus says that there is joy in heaven when a sinner repents (Luke 15:7). Saints in heaven encourage us as we run life's race toward Christ, who waits at the finish line (Hebrews 12:1). They take our prayers and offer them to God like incense (Revelation 5:8). By God's grace and power they can touch our minds and speak to our hearts. In prayer we learn to listen to God, and to God's servants, the angels and saints.

GETTING TO KNOW GOD

Real communication can happen only if people get to know one another. We might experience this, for example, when folks introduce themselves at a party. We begin to talk and gradually the new acquaintances become friends. The more we communicate, the better we get to know one another, the stronger our friendship becomes, and the more we enjoy opportunities to visit and talk. Friendship and communication build on each other.

If we want to pray, to communicate with God, we should get to know God. Fortunately, Jesus Christ has come into our world, introduced himself, and then invited us to become better acquainted with God. He did this by revealing God as Trinity. Getting to know God as Father, Son, and Holy Spirit is like getting to know other persons. But with God there is much more to get to know!

THE TRINITY

A five-year-old boy and his friends found a dead robin and decided to give it a Christian burial. They got a small box, lined it with cotton, inserted the robin, and dug a grave. The boy's father happened by and heard his son recite the burial prayer—in words the lad thought he'd heard his parents say: "Glory to the Father, and to the Son...into the hole he goes."

The boy needed clarification on the text of a traditional prayer, and instruction on the three persons of the Trinity. But it's not surprising that a five-year-old was confused about the Trinity, which names the very being of God, far beyond the reach of any human intellect.

We know of the Trinity only because Jesus revealed God as Father, Son, and Holy Spirit. The life of Jesus began when Mary was overshadowed by the Holy Spirit and conceived the "Son of God" (Luke 1:35). As Jesus was baptized in the Jordan, the Father's voice was heard and the Spirit descended as a dove (Mark 1:10). The risen Jesus told his followers to baptize "in the name of the Father and of the Son and of the Holy Spirit" (Matthew 28:19).

Jesus revealed God as Trinity because he wants to draw us into the loving embrace of the Trinity. We were created to spend eternity with God. Heaven begins here on earth when we pray and get to know God as Father, Son, and Holy Spirit.

INSIGHT INTO THE MYSTERY

We express the essentials of our belief in the Trinity every Sunday when we recite the Nicene Creed. We believe in one God: in the Father; in Jesus Christ, the only Son; in the Holy Spirit. The Son is "begotten" by the Father. The Holy Spirit "proceeds" from the Father and Son.

The *Catechism of the Catholic Church* explains that there are three persons in one divine nature (253–256). The word *person* refers to who we are. The word *nature* refers to what we are. If someone asks us, "Who are you?" we respond with our name—person. If someone asks us, "What are you?" we respond that we are human—our nature. With us there is only one person in each human nature. But with God there are three persons in one divine nature.

The word *begotten* is used in the Creed because it means that the Father and Son are of the same nature. When parents beget a child, they beget someone of the same nature as themselves. When people make something, they make something different. The Father begets the Son, but makes created things. So when we say that the Son is begotten by the Father, we profess our belief that the Son is equal to the Father, "true God from true God." When we say that the Holy Spirit "proceeds from the Father and the Son," we express the equality of the Spirit with the Father and the Son.

Further insight is possible when we remember that we are created in the image and likeness of God (Genesis 1:27). We can catch a glimpse of the Trinity by looking at ourselves. We look into a mirror and recognize our image. We know ourselves, and this knowledge is real. We love ourselves, and this love is real. God the Father knows himself from all eternity, but God's knowledge is so real, so infinitely perfect, that it is a person, the Son. The Father and Son love each other with a love so real, so infinitely perfect, that it is a person, the Holy Spirit.

It is important to realize, however, that we cannot fully understand the Trinity. We can "catch a glimpse of the Trinity by looking at ourselves," but that glimpse is very limited. Just as astronomers see only a tiny part of the universe as they look through their telescopes, so we perceive only an infinitesimal portion of God's reality. We must not think that personhood in God is modeled on our personhood. It is the opposite. Full personhood exists in God. We human beings are persons only in a limited sense. God's personhood is unlimited.

But Jesus revealed God as a Trinity of persons, as a community of love, because God wants to draw us into that community. We are destined to spend eternity with the Trinity, and heaven begins here on earth when we know God as Father, Son, and Holy Spirit.

THE FATHER

God is Father. This does not mean that God is like human fathers, but the reverse. All good qualities in human parents come from God. The Bible tells us about these qualities. God cares for us and is close to us: "...I will not forget you. / See, I have inscribed you on the palms of my hands" (Isaiah 49:15–16). God is righteous and just (Psalm 11:7; Psalm 145:17) and upholds the righteous (Psalm 37:17). But God is also compassionate and wants to forgive our sins even more than we want to be forgiven (Luke 15). God loves us beyond imagining: "I have loved you with an everlasting love" (Jeremiah 31:3). God promises that good will defeat evil and that life will conquer death: "For I am convinced that neither death, nor life...nor anything else in all creation, will be able to separate us from the love of God" (Romans 8:38–39). To these qualities Jesus adds a special note of tenderness and affection when he addresses God as "Abba," equivalent to "Dad" or "dear Father" (Mark 14:36; Romans 8:15; Galatians 4:6).

THE SON

God is Son. From all eternity, there is a relationship in God's being that we can best understand as "Father-Son." The New Testament teaches that the Son, the second person of the Trinity, became human. "In the beginning was the Word, and the Word was with God, and the Word was God....And the Word became flesh and lived among us" (John 1:1, 14).

This miracle is known as the Incarnation. It means that Jesus has a divine nature and a human nature, united in one divine person, the "Word." It was through his human nature that his contemporaries made contact with Jesus, and his human nature gives us our truest insights into the nature of God. Therefore, it is important for us to get to know Jesus well.

Jesus in his mortal life on earth was a down-to-earth human being. Raised in a small town, he seemed such a normal child that when he came back as a miracle worker, people refused to believe he was special (Mark 6:1–6). His parables show that Jesus loved nature and celebrated life: the sun and rain, wildflowers and vines and trees, moths and birds and foxes, people building houses, farmers planting crops, women baking bread, and fishermen casting their nets (Matthew 5–7, 13). He went to parties and even worked a miracle to keep a party going (John 2:1–11). He was courageous, yet experienced distress and sorrow (Mark 14:32–42). He was born like us and was willing to accept an awful death for love of us (Luke 2:1–7, chapter 23).

Jesus liked people and people liked him. He was always getting invited to meals (Luke 4:39, 7:36, 10:38, 14:1). He enjoyed being with others (John 1:35–51). He cared about little children (Mark 10:13-16) and noticed folks that others missed (Mark 10:46-52). To him elderly widows and despised sinners were important (Mark 12:41–44).

Jesus was merciful and compassionate. He defended a woman accused of adultery (John 8:1–11). He shed tears at the death of Lazarus (John 11). He wept over the fate of Jerusalem (Luke 19:41–44).

Jesus is a friend. "No one has greater love than this, to lay down one's life for one's friends. You are my friends" (John 15:13–14). When we spend time with him in prayer, as did two disciples early in his public ministry (John 1:35–42), we will enjoy getting to know him. He will lead us to the Father and give us the Spirit as helper and guide.

THE HOLY SPIRIT

God is Holy Spirit. The Spirit is love eternally proceeding from the Father and Son. This is not love in an abstract sense, but "God who loves." Jesus calls the Holy Spirit our advocate, our helper who speaks to us (John 14:16, 16:7–14). The Holy Spirit brings the power of the wind and fire that strengthened the apostles at Pentecost (Acts 2:1–4). They were weak, tainted by sin and failure, but through them the Spirit accomplished great things. Among their accomplishments was prayer so powerful that it caused the earth to tremble (Acts 4:31). "Likewise the Spirit helps us in our weakness; for we do not know how to pray as we ought, but that very Spirit intercedes with sighs too deep for words" (Romans 8:26). So the Holy Spirit helps us to pray.

When we are attentive to the presence of the Holy Spirit, we hear "that very Spirit" interceding for us. Chapter Five suggests ways of listening to the Holy Spirit, and to the Father and Son as well. For now, reflecting on what Scripture says about the Father, Son, and Holy Spirit is the best possible way to get to know God.

SCIENCE AND GOD

But Scripture is not the only way. Science studies the physical universe, and science can open our eyes to the Maker of the universe. If we study works of art, we can learn much about the artist. Likewise, Saint Paul says that we can learn much about God from created things: "Ever since the creation of the world his eternal power and divine nature, invisible though they are, have been understood and seen through the things he has made" (Romans 1:20).

This has always been so. "The heavens are telling the glory of God; / and the firmament proclaims his handiwork" (Psalm 19:1). But we are privileged to live at a time when science and technology allow us to view God's artistry in ways unimaginable in Bible times. Studying what science has learned about the vastness of the universe and the complexity of cellular life can give us a deeper appreciation of "the glory of God."

THE UNIVERSE: GOD'S HANDWORK

In a wonderful passage in the Book of Genesis, God tells Abraham that he and his wife, though advanced in years, will have a son. Abraham is dubious, so God takes him outside and tells him, "Look toward heaven and count the stars, if you are able to count them....So shall your descendants be" (Genesis 15:5). As far as we know, Abraham didn't start counting, and it's just as well. He'd still be at it, for it would take up to three thousand years to count the stars in our galaxy. Scientists tell us that there are at least one hundred billion stars in the Milky Way, perhaps as many as four hundred billion.

The stars in our galaxy would be just the beginning. There are more than one hundred billion galaxies, each with a hundred billion stars or so. And the distances in space are beyond imagining. Two friends in Dallas were discussing distances. "Which is further from Dallas?" one asked. "Florida, or the moon?" "Hello!" the other replied. "Can you see Florida from here?"

Most people, while not that confused about distances in space, have no idea of the incredible size of the universe. Science-fiction movies portray people traveling to distant galaxies in a flash. But we shouldn't expect to buy a ticket for such a trip anytime soon. Getting to the star closest to the sun from Earth would take about eighty thousand years in our fastest spaceship. We'd have to multiply that by the number of stars in the Milky Way to calculate the time needed to tour our galaxy!

That would be only the first step toward exploring the universe. Scientists use light-years to measure distance in space. Light moves at a speed of 186,282 miles per second, or roughly seven times around the world in less than a second. That's very fast. Yet, traveling from one end of the known universe to the other at the speed of light (if this were possible) would take thirty billion years. Indeed, the heavens do tell the glory of God!

"THE HAIRS OF YOUR HEAD ARE ALL COUNTED"

Jesus speaks these words to teach trust in God to his followers (Matthew 10:30). God knows us so well that even the hairs of our head are all counted, so we should be sure that God will care for us. We might think it unbelievable that God knows the number of hairs on everybody's head. If so, we have no idea of God's attention to detail.

For just as science in the past few decades has discovered the vastness of the universe, so science has discovered incredible complexity in the most minute parts of creation. In his book, *A Short History of Nearly Everything*, Bill Bryson writes:

> Every cell in nature is a thing of wonder. Even the simplest are far beyond the limits of human ingenuity. To build the most basic yeast cell, for example, you would have to miniaturize about the same number of components as are found in a Boeing 777 jetliner and fit them into a sphere just five microns across; then somehow you would have to persuade that sphere to reproduce....But yeast cells are as nothing compared with human cells... (pp. 371–72).

Scientists tell us that there are about seventy-five trillion soft tissue cells in the average adult human body. Every second, each cell produces two thousand proteins from three hundred to one thousand combinations of amino acids. And proteins are busy little workaholics. As many as a hundred million of them may be toiling away in a cell at a given moment. The total of cells in the human body is staggering; some scientists estimate the count at about ten thousand trillion.

In short, God likes details, and God likes immensity. God creates things on a scale so vast that mere human beings cannot begin to imagine their borders. God creates things so incredibly complex that scientists could spend lifetimes examining a single cell and never comprehend its makeup. Knowing the number of hairs on the heads of everybody is for God the answer to a simple trivia question!

"THROUGH THE THINGS GOD HAS MADE"

It's helpful to know a little science. When science looks into the things God has made, we all benefit. We see in these things the eternal power and divine nature that gave them being. This is important for a life of prayer. We aren't likely to seek a life of communion with God if we doubt God's existence. And doubts do arise in all of us. Some of these are probably suggested by Satan. Others come from our observing the evil in our world and the suffering of innocent people. Still others might spring from depression or fatigue.

Whatever their source, these doubts can lessen our desire to pray. But we can put the doubts to flight with an appreciation of the magnitude of the universe and the complexity of creation. Many former atheists, like Dr. Allan Sandage and Dr. Antony Flew, have become believers because scientific discoveries led them to God. If we learn more about what turned them from atheism to belief, we will more easily dismiss our own doubts and turn to God with renewed confidence and hope. (For a more detailed discussion of the relationship of science to belief, see pp. 58–65 in *The Search for Happiness*, by Oscar Lukefahr).

"HOW GREAT THOU ART"

Knowing some science can also keep us from underestimating God. We might suppose that God is just a bit smarter than the wisest human being, or just a bit more powerful than the mightiest creature on earth. Not even close. God is out of our league! The old hymn says it well: "Oh, Lord my God...how great thou art!"* But it's easy to forget.

There's a story going around about a scientist who said to God, "We scientists can do anything you can. We can even make people out of dirt." "Interesting," replied God. "Let's see you do that." The scientist bent over and grabbed a handful of dirt. "Oh, no you don't," said God. "Use your own dirt."

Scientists cannot make their own dirt. Scientists cannot make people from dirt. God can. No human being can create a galaxy. God has created over a hundred billion galaxies. We can conclude, then, not only that God is greater than any human being, but that God is at least one hundred billion times as great as any human being. And there is more to be learned from these facts than the extent of God's power. There is the extent of God's love.

Scripture tells us that God is love (1 John 4:16). Since God is at least one hundred billion times greater than any human being, God loves us at least one hundred billion times as much as any human being could. Scripture passages like Hosea 11:4 and John 15:13 cast a beautiful light on the God who calls us to prayer. When we join scientific knowledge to what we learn from Scripture, we can begin to see what a privilege it is to be given life by God and called to communion with Father, Son, and Holy Spirit.

EXCITED ABOUT PRAYING?

Imagine that the house next door to yours has been vacant for a while. You watched with interest yesterday as a moving van unloaded. A couple, just past middle age, entered the house shortly after the van arrived. Obviously, they're your new next-door neighbors. You're thinking of paying them a welcome visit when your phone rings.

It's a relative in another state who says excitedly, "Do you know who's moving next door to you? They used to live in this town. He is a retired major league baseball player who coaches Little League. She teaches home economics and loves to bake. You can't imagine how good her cherry pies are! He says he wants to keep coaching. Don't your children play ball?"

"They do," you reply. "Sounds like our new neighbors will be perfect. It'll be fun getting to know them." You hang up just as the doorbell rings. It's the new neighbors. And she is holding a cherry pie.

It *would* be fun getting to know neighbors like that. But prayer is about getting to know persons who are far more interesting and who bring more benefits than even the best of neighbors. The Father, Son, and Holy Spirit want you to enjoy their friendship. The Father, Son, and Spirit are closer than next-door neighbors. God is ever-present, any time, any place. God invites you to a "life of prayer," to "being in the presence of...God and in communion with him" (*CCC* 2565).

Jesus puts it like this: "I am standing at the door, knocking; if you hear my voice and open the door, I will come in to you and eat with you, and you with me" (Revelation 3:20).

HERE I AM, LORD!

When God called Abraham, Moses, and the prophet Samuel, their response was "Here I am, Lord." We should recapture the eagerness and anticipation they must have felt at hearing God's voice. In the remaining chapters of this book, we discover the blessings God has in store for us through prayer, and how we might best open our minds and hearts to God's presence and to those blessings. With eagerness and anticipation, we reply to God's invitation, to Jesus knocking at the door: "Here I am, Lord!"

QUESTIONS FOR DISCUSSION AND REFLECTION

Have you ever considered that prayer begins with God? The text lists many ways God speaks to us; which of these are part of your own conversations with God? What is your favorite kind of prayer? Have you ever thought that prayer could be exciting? In your opinion, can the *Catechism*'s definition of the life of prayer be realized in today's busy world? How?

ACTIVITIES

In chapters 14 through 16 of John's Gospel, Jesus spoke to his apostles at the Last Supper. He speaks the same words to you today when you read these chapters. As you read them, picture Jesus speaking the words directly to you.

Read Sirach 42:15–43:33, and prayerfully consider how this poetic description of creation can lead you to God.

Chapter Two

LORD, TEACH US
TO PRAY

꙰

Some years ago, Kyle Rote Jr., a professional soccer player in the 1970s and later a sports agent and Christian speaker, gave a talk at a prayer breakfast in southeast Missouri. He told about a friend who he would call Kyle and announce he was Oral Roberts, Tommy Lasorda, or some other famous personality. Kyle and his wife were used to this and usually laughed it off. But one day Kyle's sixty-two-year-old mother-in-law, who had heart problems, was visiting. The phone rang and she answered, then came running with the message, "It's the president of the United States." Kyle, certain that it was his friend, picked up the phone, and said, "I don't mind you playing your silly little tricks on me and my wife, but to pick on my mother-in-law is too much. Why don't you grow up!" Silence. Then a voice. It *was* President Ronald Reagan, calling to invite Kyle to speak at the White House.

How do you respond to the voice of the president? How do you respond to the voice of God? I'm sure Kyle didn't know what to say when he realized the president really was calling. What do we say when God calls?

There's a wonderful story in Scripture about a young man who didn't know God was calling. Samuel was just a lad, entrusted by his parents to the old priest, Eli, at the temple in Shiloh. One night when Samuel was sleeping in the temple, he heard someone call his name. He quickly ran to Eli and said, "Here I am, for you called me." Eli told the boy he was mistaken and should go back to sleep. This happened again, and a third time. Finally, Eli realized that God was calling Samuel. He told the lad if he heard the voice again to reply, "Speak, LORD, for your servant is listening" (1 Samuel 3:1–10).

GOD'S FIRST CALL

Samuel responded to God. Long before, however, when God called the first human beings, they tried to ignore God's voice. Adam and Eve disobeyed God and hid in their garden. God kept calling: "Where are you?" Shamefacedly, they owned up to their sin, accepted due punishment, and were promised redemption (Genesis 3).

Down through the ages, human beings have responded to God's call in many ways—from the silence of Adam and Eve to Samuel's eager reply. How do we recognize God's voice? How shall we respond to the many ways God calls out to us? The Bible is an invaluable source of answers to these questions.

The Bible is a collection of forty-six books written before Christ—the Old Testament, and twenty-seven books written after Christ's resurrection—the New Testament. The Catholic Church teaches that all these books are divinely inspired, that they have God as author. This does not mean that God dictated the books, but that God guided the human authors to write in such a way that the books teach without error the truths necessary for salvation. Because the Bible has God as author, it has an integrity and power found in no other literature. Because the Bible has human beings as authors, it has limitations traceable to human weakness and frailty.

The Bible honestly addresses every human situation, reflects every emotion, and paints vivid pictures of all kinds of people. It is great literature that shows how human beings, good and bad, have related to God since they were created. As we read their stories, we learn more about who God really is. We discover ways to enter into dialogue with the living God.

GOD KEEPS CALLING

God is love, and he was not discouraged by the sin of Adam and Eve. God continued to address every human being in the act of giving life, in the beauty of creation, in quiet words spoken to the heart. When anyone listened, communication with God occurred.

Scripture says that God chastened Cain, a son of Adam and Eve, for murdering his brother, Abel (Genesis 4:1–16). When sin inundated the world in a flood of wickedness, God instructed Noah to build an ark where he and his family would find safety. God and Noah made a covenant, an agreement whereby God promised to care for Noah, who pledged faithful service to God (Genesis 6–9). Only God knows how many other conversations took place between God and humanity in the millennia that followed, how often God was ignored, how often people found solace and hope in the life of prayer.

The Book of Genesis resumes its history of prayer with Abram, a native of Ur, an ancient city north of the Persian Gulf. About 1900 BC, Abram's family migrated to Haran, a city near the present-day Turkish-Syrian border. In Haran, Abram received a call from God to move to Canaan, present-day Palestine. God made a covenant with Abram, changing his name to Abraham and promising that he and his wife, Sarah, would have a son, the first in a long line of descendants. They would be called Hebrews, as was Abraham (Genesis 14:13), and would also be known as Israelites and Jews. God spoke to Abraham in visions, in the majesty of the universe, in heart-to-heart conversations, in a lively bargaining session, in ritual sacrifice, and in covenant promises (Genesis 13–25). Conversations continued between God and Abraham's descendants—Isaac, Jacob, and Jacob's sons (Genesis

26–50). When Joseph, one of those sons, became a prominent leader in Egypt, Jacob and the rest of his family migrated there about 1720 BC.

Centuries passed, and their descendants became slaves in Egypt. Around 1250 BC God called again.

BURNING BUSHES AND FIRE ON THE ALTAR

Some time ago I read a story by a gentleman who frequently took morning walks. As he neared his parish church one day, he noticed that some shrubbery was on fire, probably from a carelessly tossed cigarette. He quickly rang the doorbell and told the secretary to notify the fire department. She called, identified herself, gave the location, and explained the situation. "You mean to tell me," said the emergency dispatcher, "that there's a burning bush on your church lawn, and you want to put it out?"

It was at a burning bush, as most of us know, that God spoke to Moses, a Hebrew who was raised in Egypt's royal palace and later had to flee for his life. In the desert Moses saw a bush aflame, but not consumed. He approached to examine this marvel (not to put out the fire!). God spoke from the bush and a conversation began that would change the world.

God directed Moses to lead the Israelites from slavery in Egypt to freedom in the land of Canaan (the territory known at various times as the Promised Land, Israel, Judah, Judea, Palestine, and the Holy Land). God made this possible by events the Jews would recall in their annual Passover meal (Exodus 1–13). Moses encountered God in the crossing of the Red Sea (Exodus 14), in the thunder of Mount Sinai (Exodus 20), and in the intimacy of the meeting tent (Exodus 33). Moses was for the Israelites a living proof that prayer with the true God could express every human emotion. He showed gratitude (Exodus 15), he pleaded (Exodus 17), he complained (Numbers 11), and he interceded (Numbers 14).

The Bible speaks of the Ten Commandments as given by God to Moses (Exodus 34). It names Moses as the religious leader who designed the Ark of the Covenant, a portable chest that contained the Ten Commandments and formed the throne where God met the Israelites. Moses, then, was the leader who put the Israelites back in touch with God.

It was to Moses, the Israelites believed, that God gave the law, not just the Ten Commandments, but all the traditional practices of Judaism and the guidelines for religious observances (Leviticus). The Jews looked to Moses as the founder of their communal worship, the sacrificial holocausts, wherein animals consumed by fire expressed utter dependence upon the Lord. Moses was for the Jewish people also the model of intimate communion with God: "Thus the LORD used to speak to Moses face to face, as one speaks to a friend" (Exodus 33:11).

THE PROMISED LAND

Moses died on the border of the Promised Land, and his lieutenant, Joshua, led the people into Canaan about 1210 BC. There followed a period of conquest, with the twelve tribes (divisions of the Hebrew people named after the sons of Jacob) settling in various parts of Canaan. After Joshua's death, the Israelites fought with the inhabitants (Philistines and others) through a long frontier period called the Time of the Judges. This was a harsh and ruthless epoch when the Israelites and their pagan neighbors engaged in bloody struggles for survival. Life among the Israelites was marked with intrigue, treachery, murder, and civil conflict.

God never abandoned the Israelites, even when they tested God's promises to the limit. The story of Gideon and his fleece is well known, but we should not miss the point of God's graciousness in catering to Gideon's requests (Judges 6:37–40). While God's goodness never ceased, humanity's sinfulness sank to such depths that even religious vows became perverse, as when Jephthah offered his daughter as a holocaust (Judges 11:29–40).

The Book of Judges paints a macabre picture of humanity at its worst and of what happens to those who abandon God. About 1020 BC Saul, a member of the tribe of Benjamin, began to bring the tribes together and was named king. But he too fell away from the Lord, went insane, and was killed in a battle with the Philistines. Into the breach stepped David, a young military leader who soon became king.

THE PSALMS AND THE TEMPLE

If the Time of the Judges and the life of Saul showed humanity's need for God, the reign of David indicated how God can raise individuals and nations from the depths. David himself fell into grave sin when he committed adultery with a woman named Bathsheba, then murdered her husband, one of his most loyal soldiers. But David heard God calling him to repentance and responded with prayer, fasting, and penance (2 Samuel 12). Beginning about 1000 BC, David united the tribes, set up Jerusalem as the center of his government, defeated the enemies of the Israelites, and made Israel a force to be reckoned with in the Middle East.

Before David became a soldier, he was a shepherd and musician. He is renowned as the founder of the Israelite psalm tradition. Psalms are works of poetry that were set to music, and one hundred fifty of them are collected in the biblical Book of Psalms. The oldest are dated at least to David's reign, and the most recent to the fourth century before Christ. More than half the psalms are attributed to David, others to individuals like Moses or to groups such as the Korahites, song leaders at worship. David surely authored some of the psalms, but others may have been written by anonymous authors who used the great king's name as an expression of their desire to write as David did.

David wanted to build a temple in Jerusalem to house the

Ark of the Covenant. But this task was accomplished by his son, Solomon, who constructed a magnificent edifice. Here, Solomon led his people in public prayer of praise and petition (1 Kings 8), and here the psalms became a centerpiece of Jewish worship.

PRAYING THE PSALMS

Jesus himself prayed the psalms at temple and synagogue services. He quoted the psalms in his teaching (Luke 20:42), and the Book of Psalms would have been his "prayer book." From the earliest days of Christianity, the psalms were used in worship. They are the heart of The Liturgy of the Hours, the official prayer of the Church (see chapter 5). Catholics recite portions of the psalms at Mass and other liturgical functions. In imitation of Jesus, many Catholics use the Book of Psalms as a resource for private prayer.

The psalms were written more than two thousand years ago for Jews, yet they have been prayed by believers of every age, nation, and culture and remain popular today. One reason for their popularity is that they deal with human feelings and give us words to express our emotions to God. Being general in tone, they allow us to fit our particular circumstances into their framework. The psalms thus show that the emotional side of human nature is an integral part of our relationship with God. They also allow us to stand before God, not just as isolated individuals, but as members of the community of believers who have prayed them through the centuries and who pray with us today.

THE PSALMS AS POETRY

The poetry of the psalms is not based on rhyme or meter. Instead, Hebrew poetry depends on the balance of ideas. We must admire God's careful planning here. God's inspired word in the Scriptures is meant for people of every nationality and language.

Poetry based on rhyme or meter would be difficult to translate, whereas poetry based on the balance of ideas can be expressed in any tongue.

The Jews developed their poetry by establishing certain patterns of thought. When we become aware of these patterns, we better appreciate the music of the psalms. Scholars distinguish many different types of patterns, but we can understand and enjoy the poetry by noting just a few of these.

The most common pattern is *repetition*, where similar ideas are expressed in different words:

> *Give ear to my words, O LORD;*
> *give heed to my sighing* (Psalm 5:1).

Another pattern frequently used is *contrast*, where dissimilar ideas are compared:

> *The young lions suffer want and hunger,*
> *but those who seek the LORD lack no good thing*
> (Psalm 34:10).

A third pattern may be called *construction*; here, ideas are built upon one another:

> *Your steadfast love, O LORD, extends to the heavens,*
> *your faithfulness to the clouds.*
> *Your righteousness is like the mighty mountains,*
> *your judgments are like the great deep;*
> *you save humans and animals alike, O LORD*
> (Psalm 36:5–6).

Knowing these patterns, we can enjoy the flow and balance of ideas in Hebrew poetry, and more readily understand and appreciate the psalms. A good way to make the psalms our own is to read through them all, keeping a list of those most appealing for prayer and reflection.

When we pray the psalms, it is often helpful to adapt them to our own situation. For example, Psalm 23 will have one meaning if we use it before setting out on a long journey and another if we pray it while waiting for the results of a medical test.

The psalms can be powerful intercessory prayers, especially when we pray them for another as if we were that person. In praying Psalm 6, for instance, we may not be feeling the distress and anguish verbalized there, but we may know a friend who is experiencing sorrow. We may pray Psalm 6 in the name of that friend, who through our prayer can be touched by God's grace.

The psalms, of course, antedate the teaching of Jesus and they have limitations. Some reflect a spirit of vengeance: "O God, break the teeth in their mouths" (Psalm 58:6), and a spirit of cruelty: "O daughter Babylon, you devastator! / Happy shall they be who pay you back... / who take your little ones / and dash them against the rock!" (Psalm 137:8–9). Some of the most wonderful psalms, like Psalm 139, have passages that may not be in keeping with the forgiveness and mercy of Christ (verses 19–22). We may skip over such passages in our prayer, focusing instead on those that reflect the sentiments of Jesus and best imitate his prayer, which we study later in this chapter.

WISDOM AND PRAYER

The Book of Psalms is classified among the seven wisdom books of the Old Testament. Many ancient cultures had collections of wise sayings, poetry, proverbs, drama, and song. Jewish wisdom, however, was unique in the way it reflected a distinctive belief in God and in a moral order based on God's will. In the seven wisdom books we find advice about relating to God, attitudes of humility, reverence, and love for our Creator, as well as examples of prayer.

Among my favorite prayers from the wisdom books are Sirach's meditation on God's majesty and mercy (18:1–14), his reflection on God's creative power (39:12–35), and his magnificent song praising God's works in nature (42:15–43:33).

The Book of Job deserves attention. In ancient times, as in our own, some people felt that suffering was always divine punishment for personal sinfulness. Those who suffered needed to repent, pray with faith, and they would be healed. The Book of Job is a powerful drama designed to counter these false attitudes and to examine the meaning of suffering. Job is afflicted with terrible sufferings. Friends explain this as punishment for his past sins. Job knows this is not so, but he errs by demanding that God give reasons for his suffering.

The drama comes to a climax when God appears on the scene to confront Job. "Who are you to question me? Could you create the universe? Do you govern the stars? Are you master of life? Can you control the power of wild beasts?" Job is overwhelmed. "I know that you can do all things," he whispers. "...I have uttered what I did not understand.... / I had heard of you by the hearing of the ear, / but now my eye sees you; / therefore I despise myself, / and repent in dust and ashes" (Job 42:2–6). Then God reproves Job's friends for their arrogance, and blesses Job by restoring his health and possessions.

The story of Job has two important morals. First, we ought not try to bring God down to our level by offering simplistic answers to life's greatest problems. To presume, on one hand, as Job's friends did, that all suffering must be punishment from God is an insult to the Lord. To presume, on the other hand, as Job did, that we can understand all life's mysteries is foolish. Second, when we are suffering, only an encounter with the Lord can bring us peace.

The Book of Job is a drama. But behind it, no doubt, is a real story of anguish. Its author may have been stricken with a mortal illness. His friends perhaps suggested that if he prayed with faith, all would be well. Then the author felt God's presence in some powerful way, perhaps through a near-death experience, and this brought peace.

The Book of Job encourages us to seek God in prayer in times of pain and desolation. It helps us realize that while there is no easy answer to the problem of suffering, there is an answer. It is the faith-realization that the Lord is near and that we can entrust ourselves to God's loving care. When we pray with Job, "I have uttered what I did not understand…but now my eye sees you" (42:3, 5), we are on a journey that will lead us to Jesus. Jesus knew pain more terrible than Job's and cried out from the cross, "My God, my God, why have you forsaken me?" (Mark 15:34). But in his pain he experienced God's presence and loving care: "Father, into your hands I commend my spirit" (Luke 23:46). When we begin with Job, we are led to Jesus on prayer's pathway to peace.

THE PROPHETS

The word *prophet* means "someone who speaks for another." Old Testament prophets were those who spoke for God. The Jewish people and their leaders often failed to keep the commandments handed down through Moses. God inspired prophets to speak out against such failures, to remind people of the covenant, and to call them to repentance. The prophets advised rulers, taught morality, warned sinners, threatened evildoers, and consoled the suffering. God spoke through them. Their expression, "Thus says the Lord," is found 417 times in the Old Testament. What God said then about justice, truth, righteousness, and love, God says to us today in the prophetic books.

In these books, we hear God speaking words of remarkable tenderness and affection:

Can a woman forget her nursing child,
   or show no compassion for the child of her womb?
Even these may forget,
   yet I will not forget you.
See, I have inscribed you on the palms of my hands"
(Isaiah 49:15–16).

"I have loved you with an everlasting love"
(Jeremiah 31:3).

God also makes demands. "Seek good and not evil, / that you may live; / and so the LORD, the God of hosts, will be with you" (Amos 5:14). Sin brings down a terrible judgment. "Woe to the guilty! How unfortunate they are, / for what their hands have done shall be done to them" (Isaiah 3:11).

But there is hope for those who repent. God's mercy and compassion are everlasting:

The days are surely coming, says the LORD, when I will make a new covenant with the house of Israel and the house of Judah. It will not be like the covenant that I made with their ancestors when I took them by the hand to bring them out of the land of Egypt—a covenant that they broke, though I was their husband, says the LORD. But this is the covenant that I will make with the house of Israel after those days, says the LORD: I will put my law within them, and I will write it on their hearts; and I will be their God, and they shall be my people (Jeremiah 31:31–33).

The prophets listened to God, and responded. At times they spoke with awe and reverence. "Holy, holy, holy is the LORD of hosts; / the whole earth is full of his glory" (Isaiah 6:3). They joined all creation in praising God: "Bless the Lord, all you works of the Lord" (Daniel 3:57). At times they cried out in anger and frustration. "O LORD...you have overpowered me, / and you have prevailed. / I have become a laughingstock all day long; / everyone mocks me.... / For the word of the LORD has become for me /a reproach and derision all day long" (Jeremiah 20:7–8). We learn from the prophets that we can be honest with God. Whatever our feelings, we can express them to the Lord.

HOPE FOR THE FUTURE

The history of the Jewish people after Solomon was marked by tragedy: civil conflict, defeat in war, exile, and submission to Greek, Syrian, and Roman overlords. Through it all, the prophets spoke for God and delivered a message of hope. They foretold that God would send salvation, a messiah, a savior.

In modern versions of the Bible, the prophetic books close the Old Testament. Its final words are spoken by God in the Book of the prophet Malachi. They are words that recognize the drama and weakness of humanity, but they are also words of hope. "Lo, I will send you the prophet Elijah before the great and terrible day of the LORD comes. He will turn the hearts of parents to their children and the hearts of children to their parents, so that I will not come and strike the land with a curse" (Malachi 4:5–6).

There would be a savior. The dialogue between God and humanity would continue in a way no one could have imagined. God would become one of us.

HOPE REALIZED IN JESUS CHRIST

Jesus Christ, born of the Virgin Mary by the power of the Holy Spirit, is truly God and truly human. Because he is divine, every word he speaks in Scripture is spoken by God. So if we want to hear God speaking, we don't have to wait for voices from heaven. All we have to do is pick up our Bible and read the words of Jesus.

Of special importance are words of hope Jesus spoke in answer to the prayers and needs of believers. In the storms of life, Jesus says to us, as he did to the apostles on the raging sea: "Take heart, it is I; do not be afraid" (Matthew 14:27). When we are discouraged or depressed, Jesus comforts us: "Peace I leave with you; my peace I give to you. I do not give to you as the world gives. Do not let your hearts be troubled, and do not let them be afraid" (John 14:27).

Sooner or later, we all need to hear the language of hope and peace. Father John, who had served in various parts of the world during his more than sixty years as a priest, spent his last years in a retirement home for clergy. One day he woke up speaking only French. None of the health-care workers could speak the language, so they just cared for him as usual. But one of the ladies on the evening shift knew French, and she responded to him in that language. Father John asked, *"Parlez-vous français?"* When she answered in the affirmative, he asked, *"Parlez-vous anglais?* Do you speak English?" She responded, *"Oui! Mon Père.* Of course, I do, Father." Father John replied, "Thank God, I've been trying to find somebody all day who can speak English!"

Father John wanted someone who could speak the language of English. We want someone who can speak the language of hope. That someone is Jesus Christ. He speaks the language of hope in the words just quoted and throughout the gospels. But he does so most clearly on the night before he died. When we are given a share in the passion of Christ, when we must take up the cross and follow Jesus, we should turn to chapters 14 to 17 of the Gospel of John. There we will find the language of hope!

THE PRAYER OF JESUS

We can never fully grasp the mystery of Jesus' prayer, but we can be sure that Jesus' divinity did not negate his humanity. Jesus "increased in wisdom and in years, and in divine and human favor" (Luke 2:52). Prayer must have been a part of the process by which he knew God as his Father (Luke 2:49) and himself as God's beloved Son (Luke 3:22). Jesus prayed for the same reason we do: to communicate with God. But his prayer was perfect, and so, like the apostles, we turn to him and ask, "Lord, teach us to pray" (Luke 11:1).

Prayer was as natural to Jesus as breathing. He began his public life with prayer (Luke 3:21), then went into the desert to spend forty days in communion with God (Matthew 4:1–11). He prayed often and long during his ministry, even at the busiest times (Mark 1:35, 6:45). He prayed before making important decisions, like choosing the Twelve Apostles (Luke 6:12–16). His union with his Father could be so intense that it left his disciples awestruck (Luke 9:28–36). He prayed for himself "with loud cries and tears" (Hebrews 5:7–8), and he prayed for his apostles (Luke 22:31).

Even as a child, Jesus worshiped in the Jerusalem Temple (Luke 2:41–51). He prayed in synagogues, where he read the Scriptures and taught (Luke 4:16–27). He participated in Jewish worship, praying and singing with his apostles (Mark 14:12–26).

PRAYING IN JESUS' OWN WORDS

Some humorist remarked, "I'm afraid someday I'll meet God. He'll sneeze, and I won't know what to say to him." If we wonder what to say to God, we can pray in Jesus' own words recorded in the New Testament.

First and foremost is the prayer Jesus taught us, the "Lord's Prayer" (see Matthew 6:9–13). This prayer is simple. It has been memorized by small children and uttered as the last words of the dying. Yet it has a depth of meaning that will be plumbed until the end of time. The *Catechism of the Catholic Church* calls it "the summary of the whole gospel" and offers a fine explanation of each of its phrases (2759–2865).

In other chapters, we discuss various forms of prayer such as adoration, thanks, and petition. The prayers of Jesus are models for each of these forms. Jesus praised God for having revealed his mysteries to the childlike (Matthew 11:25–26), thanked God just before he raised Lazarus from the dead (John 11:41–42), and interceded for the disciples and for us (John 17). When troubled, Jesus prayed to his Father (John 12:27–28), and in his agony he prayed at Gethsemane (Matthew 26:36–44). In prayers said from the cross, Jesus forgave those who persecuted him (Luke 23:34), expressed feelings of desolation (Matthew 27:46), and commended his spirit into the hands of his Father (Luke 23:46).

TEACHINGS ABOUT PRAYER

Looking beyond the actual prayers said by Jesus, we find that he taught a great deal about prayer. In the Sermon on the Mount, Jesus tells us that we must pray with sincerity, not to impress others. We must avoid the pagan attitude that God owes us a response in proportion to the length of our prayers (Matthew 6:5–8). Our Father knows what we need before we ask. But prayer expresses our dependence on God and helps us put God's kingdom first (Matthew 6:32–33). Prerequisites for prayer are humility (Luke 18:9–14) and forgiveness of others (Mark 11: 25–26).

Jesus asks us to pray for more laborers in the Lord's harvest (Luke 10:2). He tells the apostles, and us, to pray that we not "come into the time of trial" (Mark 14:38). He invites us to approach him in prayer. "Come to me, all you that are weary and are carrying heavy burdens, and I will give you rest. Take my yoke upon you, and learn from me; for I am gentle and humble in heart, and you will find rest for your souls. For my yoke is easy, and my burden is light" (Matthew 11:28–30).

We should pray with faith and confidence, for prayer is always answered. "I will do whatever you ask in my name" (John 14:13). "So I tell you, whatever you ask for in prayer, believe that you have received it, and it will be yours" (Mark 11:24). "Ask, and it will be given you; search, and you will find; knock, and the door will be opened for you" (Matthew 7:7). There is a special power in common prayer: "Again, truly I tell you, if two of you agree on earth about anything you ask, it will be done for you by my Father in heaven" (Matthew 18:19).

If we read only the passages in the previous paragraph, however, we can get a one-sided view of Jesus' teaching on prayer. We've all had the experience of asking and *not* being given what we want. Because of this we may get discouraged and stop praying, or we might feel guilty, thinking we lack faith. But these passages must be interpreted in the light of Jesus' other teachings about prayer.

Jesus implies that God's answer to prayer may take time, for perseverance in prayer is necessary (Luke 11:5–13; 18:1–8). Jesus also shows us that our prayer must always be made in accordance with God's will. In the Garden of Gethsemane, Jesus prayed, "My Father, if it is possible, let this cup pass from me; yet not what I want but what you want" (Matthew 26:39). "Thy will be done" must be the foundation of any prayer we say.

The perfect submission of Jesus to God's will was part of his every prayer. Jesus promises to do whatever we ask in his name. Asking in Jesus' name means praying as Jesus did, always with the condition, "If this is God's will." Jesus says, "If you abide in me, and my words abide in you, ask for whatever you wish, and it will be done for you" (John 15:7). If we abide in Jesus, we must endure with him the agony of Gethsemane. We must take up the cross and follow him. And if the words of Jesus abide in us, we must pray to the Father as he did: "Not as I will, but as you will." Prayer is always answered, but not always in the way we want.

OTHER GOSPEL PRAYERS

Just as we can pray in the words of Jesus, so we can pray in the words of the people who knew him. These prayers have a special value because they are inspired by God. Three of them, placed on the lips of Mary (Luke 1:46–55), Zechariah (Luke 1:68–79), and Simeon (Luke 2:29–32) are used in the Liturgy of the Hours. Mary's prayer is a hymn of praise to God for showering graces on her, a humble servant of the Lord. Zechariah's prophecy glorifies God for raising up a Savior whose way would be prepared by Zechariah's son, John. Simeon expresses his readiness to go in peace, for he has seen the salvation promised by God.

A prayer especially dear to Catholics, the Hail Mary, is rooted in the New Testament. Its opening words are spoken by Gabriel to Mary: "Greetings, favored one! The Lord is with you" (Luke 1:28). The next phrases come from Elizabeth's joyful welcome to Mary: "Blessed are you among women, and blessed is the fruit of your womb" (Luke 1:42).

We can make our own the brief prayers found throughout the gospels. They may be used to praise and adore God: "Glory to God in the highest heaven, / and on earth peace among those whom he favors!" (Luke 2:14). "You are the Messiah, the Son of the living God" (Matthew 16:16). "Lord, it is good for us to be here" (Matthew 17:4). "Hosanna to the Son of David! / Blessed is the one who comes in the name of the Lord! / Hosanna in the highest heaven!" (Matthew 21:9). "Lord, to whom shall we go? You have the words of eternal life" (John 6:68). "My Lord and my God!" (John 20:28). "Lord, you know everything; you know that I love you" (John 21:17).

There are prayers of sorrow and contrition: "Lord, if you choose, you can make me clean" (Matthew 8:2). "Lord, I am not worthy to have you come under my roof" (Matthew 8:8). "God, be merciful to me, a sinner!" (Luke 18:13).

There are prayers of petition: "Lord, save us! We are perish-
ing!" (Matthew 8:25). "Lord, save me" (Matthew 14:30). "Have
mercy on me, Lord, Son of David" (Matthew 15:22). "Lord, help
me" (Matthew 15:25). "Lord, have mercy on my son" (Matthew
17:14). "Lord, have mercy on us" (Matthew 20:30). "Lord, let our
eyes be opened" (Matthew 20:33). "I believe; help my unbelief"
(Mark 9:24). "Lord, teach us to pray" (Luke 11:1). "Increase our
faith" (Luke 17:5). "Jesus, remember me when you come into your
kingdom" (Luke 23:42). "Lord, I believe" (John 9:38). "Lord,
show us the Father, and we will be satisfied" (John 14:8).

WORSHIP RENEWED

Jesus said that he had come to fulfill the prophets (Matthew
5:17). When he saw his Father's house being desecrated, he drove
out the moneychangers and sellers (Matthew 21:12). He foretold
that the Temple would be destroyed (Matthew 24:1–2) and that
a new Temple, his own body, would be raised up (John 2:19–21).
He replaced the Passover with the Lord's Supper, and told his
apostles, "Do this in remembrance of me" (Luke 22:14–20). In
this supper, and in all the sacred actions he gave to his Church,
the sacraments, Jesus raised prayer and worship to a new level.
The sacraments as prayer are worthy of special attention, and we
study them in Chapter Six.

OTHER NEW TESTAMENT
TEACHINGS ABOUT PRAYER

From the New Testament we learn how to pray in the spirit of
the first Christians. Prayer is, above all, Trinitarian. God is to be
addressed personally as our dear Father (Romans 8:15). We pray
to the Father "through Jesus Christ" (Romans 1:8), who always
intercedes for us (Hebrews 7:25). The Holy Spirit lives in us and
helps us to pray; "the Spirit helps us in our weakness; for we do

not know how to pray as we ought, but that very Spirit intercedes with sighs too deep for words" (Romans 8:26).

The New Testament encourages us to pray at all times (Ephesians 6:18), in common with others (Acts 2:42), and in song (Colossians 3:16). Prayer may be praise (Romans 14:11), thanks (Colossians 3:17), sorrow for sin (James 5:16), and petition (Philippians 4:6). Prayer intentions include safe travel (Romans 1:10), salvation of others (Romans 10:1), deliverance from enemies (Romans 15:31), spiritual needs (Ephesians 3:14–21), and peace (1 Timothy 2:1–4). In time of special need, fasting may accompany prayer (Acts 13:2–3; 14:23).

Paul gives us beautiful prayers (Romans 11:33–36; 2 Corinthians 1:3–4; 1 Thessalonians 3:12–13) and magnificent hymns of praise (Ephesians 1:3–10; Philippians 2:5–11; Colossians 1:12–20). There are many other prayers to be found in the New Testament; see for example, 1 Peter 1:3–5; Revelation 4:11; 11:17–18; 15:3–4; 19:1–8.

One way to deepen our prayer life, in fact, is to read the entire New Testament, noting those prayers and teachings about prayer that are especially meaningful to us. We may return to these often. When we wonder how to talk to God, we turn to Jesus and ask, "Lord, teach us to pray." In the Old Testament, understood in the light of the gospel, and in the New Testament he inspired, Jesus answers our request. He tells us what to say when God calls.

QUESTIONS FOR
DISCUSSION AND REFLECTION

The *Catechism of the Catholic Church* says this about Scripture and prayer:

> In Sacred Scripture, the Church constantly finds her nourishment and her strength, for she welcomes it not as a human word, "but as what it really is, the word of God." "In the sacred books, the Father who is in heaven comes lovingly to meet his children, and talks with them" (104).

How do you see these words reflected in this chapter? In what ways does the Father lovingly meet and talk with us in the sacred books?

> Still, the Christian faith is not a "religion of the book." Christianity is the religion of the "Word" of God..."not a written and mute word, but...incarnate and living." If the Scriptures are not to remain a dead letter, Christ, the eternal Word of the living God, must, through the Holy Spirit, "open [our] minds to understand the Scriptures" (CCC 108).

Many passages in the Bible are difficult to understand. For example, did God really tell Jewish military leaders to wipe out all the men, women, and children in hostile cities? How are we to understand such prayers as Psalms 58 and 137? What is your opinion about such passages? What is the Catholic way of interpreting these passages? In what way does Christ, through the Holy Spirit, open our minds to understand the Scriptures? (If you have not studied the Bible in detail or considered these questions, you might want to read *A Catholic Guide to the Bible*, as listed in the bibliography.)

Have you thought of the Bible as a resource for personal prayer? What is your favorite psalm? What is your favorite prayer from the Old Testament? From the New Testament? (If you don't have a favorite from the Old Testament, check out Sirach 18:1–14; 39:12–35; and 42:15—43:33, or try Daniel 3:57–97. If you don't have a favorite from the New Testament, review the many prayers previously listed.)

ACTIVITIES

Find a quiet place and time. Ask God to speak to you, then listen to God's voice, using some of the Bible passages cited above. Quietly reflect on these passages. Then respond, again using some of the suggested prayers listed in this chapter.

Chapter Three

"ACTS" OF PRAYER

⟨—✦—⟩

Earth's crammed with heaven,
And every common bush afire with God:
But only he who sees, takes off his shoes,
The rest sit round it and pluck blackberries,
And daub their natural faces unaware.
ELIZABETH BARRETT BROWNING, *AURORA LEIGH*

I've often been asked, "Why did God speak only to the Jews, to people like Moses and Abraham?" Elizabeth Barrett Browning's insightful lines suggest the answer. God did not speak only to the Jews. God speaks to every human being, but only those who see a bush afire with God take off their shoes to listen and reply.

In the first chapter we reflected on the many ways that God addresses us. In the second we studied what the Bible has to say about prayer. All this information can be overwhelming. Is there a simple way to get to the essentials of prayer?

A few years ago, a young couple called me for an appointment. They were expecting their second child, and they'd just learned that the child had serious heart problems. The baby, a girl, might not survive until birth. If she did, immediate surgery, difficult and dangerous, would be required. If she lived, two more open-heart operations would be needed within a few years. It was a frightening situation, and we talked about it for a long while. As our meeting drew to a close, I promised prayers and asked them to pray together every day. "But Father," they asked, "How do we pray?"

A burning bush not of their own choosing had suddenly appeared before them. They needed, like Moses, to find God in the fire, to listen, and to respond. So it is with all of us. When we see a bush aflame with God's presence, how do we pray? What is prayer? What are the essentials of prayer?

"ACTS" OF PRAYER

The *Catechism of the Catholic Church* offers a traditional definition of prayer as "the raising of one's mind and heart to God" (2559). The question of how to raise the mind and heart to God has often been answered by recognizing four divisions of prayer. I learned them many years ago and have found them helpful as the four essential ways of relating to God. They are *a*doration, *c*ontrition, *t*hanksgiving, and *s*upplication. The word *ACTS* can help us remember these basic divisions.

Prayer is *A*doration—worshiping and praising God as the Supreme Being from whom everything receives its existence.

Prayer is *C*ontrition—expressing sorrow for our sins and failings, recognizing God as a loving savior who understands our weakness and lifts us up when we fall.

Prayer is *T*hanksgiving—recognizing God as the source of all that is good, expressing gratitude for God's countless blessings.

Prayer is *S*upplication—petition, asking God for what we need.

UNION AND FRIENDSHIP WITH GOD

We saw in Chapter One that God calls us to a life of union with him. Jesus tells us that we are his friends. The four kinds of prayer may be understood as ways of deepening our union with God and our friendship with Jesus.

Human friends recognize the good in one another. Adoration is our way of recognizing the unique goodness of God.

Because we are human, even the best of friends have faults and failings. When we express regret for our faults and are forgiven, friendship is strengthened. Contrition is expressing regret to God for our failings and asking God's forgiveness.

Friends do favors for one another and readily express gratitude for favors done. Thanksgiving recognizes the blessings that flow endlessly from God and expresses gratitude to God.

We turn to friends when we are in need and, because we trust them, we ask for help. Supplication turns us toward God with confidence that God will hear and grant our petitions.

In this chapter we study adoration, contrition, and thanksgiving. In the next we will examine supplication.

ADORATION

Our first reaction to greatness in others is usually admiration. I remember being at a concert where a young girl played the violin with exceptional skill. We applauded after each number, gave a standing ovation at the close, then talked about her performance for some time. Baseball fans jump up and cheer when a home run puts their team ahead. They may keep up their applause until the batter comes out of the dugout and takes a bow. If we have the opportunity to talk to musicians or athletes after a great performance, we congratulate them and express admiration.

God's accomplishments go far beyond any human achievement. So it's not surprising that when we enter God's presence, our first reaction is adoration.

> *When I look at your heavens, the work of your fingers,*
> *the moon and the stars that you have established;*
> *what are human beings that you are mindful of them,*
> *mortals that you care for them?* (Psalm 8:3–4).

But what is even more wonderful is that God does care about us. Many famous personalities consider themselves above ordinary people. They surround themselves with bodyguards and isolate themselves behind iron gates. Not God! God never ignores ordinary people. God's greatness is not something to be carefully guarded and kept from others. It is so expansive that it is shared with us. Psalm 8 continues:

> *Yet you have made them a little lower than God,*
> *and crowned them with glory and honor.*
> *You have given them dominion over the*
> *works of your hands;*
> *you have put all things under their feet (5–6).*

WHY WE ADORE GOD

We must recognize the true purpose of adoration. It benefits us, not God. Actors and athletes thrive on praise. They need applause for reassurance. But this is not the case with God. God is perfect and needs nothing. God does not benefit from our acclaim. We do.

People who appreciate a magnificent painting are enriched by its beauty. Football fans are thrilled when their team wins the Super Bowl. When we appreciate the artwork of God's creation, we are enriched beyond measure. When we recall Christ's victory over sin and death at his resurrection, we are blessed with joy and peace.

Adoration is essential to happy living, because it helps us to live in the real world. In our materialistic society, we can be led to think that happiness comes from possessions. Advertising encourages us to suppose that we will find fulfillment in a new car, in clothing, or in a bigger boat. We can scramble through life, always wanting more and never being satisfied. God, Saint Augustine remarked, has made us for himself, and our hearts are restless until they rest in him. Adoration helps us to see God as our origin and our ultimate goal. *This* is the real world!

WORDS OF ADORATION IN THE BIBLE

The Bible is our best source for prayers of adoration. The Book of Psalms is filled with hymns of praise. Psalm 117, brief and easily memorized, is a favorite of many. The last six psalms are beautiful prayers of adoration and praise. In the New Testament, the prayer of Zechariah is a great hymn of praise (Luke 1:68–79). Angels show us how to praise God in Luke 2:14: "Glory to God in the highest heaven." Matthew 21:9 offers an inspired prayer of praise to Jesus: "Hosanna to the Son of David! / Blessed is the one who comes in the name of the Lord! / Hosanna in the highest heaven!"

Three biblical words of praise found in the Old and New Testaments and used in Catholic liturgical prayer and hymns are "Alleluia," "Amen," and "Hosanna." *Alleluia* is a Latin transcription of the Hebrew word *Hallelujah,* meaning "Praised be the One who is." Perhaps the oldest word of praise to the one God, it is used in the *New American Bible*, while in the *New Revised Standard Bible* it is translated as "Praise the Lord" or kept in the Hebrew form, "Hallelujah." (See, for example, Psalm 104:35 and Revelation 19:1.) *Alleluia* is used frequently at Mass and in many hymns and prayers. It serves well any time as a one-word prayer of praise to God.

Amen is a Hebrew word that means "So be it." It is used to conclude many Catholic prayers in liturgy and elsewhere. Individuals sometimes say "Amen" to phrases they want to affirm. In Revelation 3:14, Jesus himself is called "the Amen, the faithful and true witness, the origin of God's creation." The word is so commonly used that it can seem to be no more than a period at the end of a sentence. I love the true story about a little boy who by the age of two learned that prayers ended with "Amen." At a church service, he got tired of a long prayer by one of the petitioners and politely said, "Amen." But the prayer did not stop. He must have had enough, because in a little while he shouted, "I said *'Amen!'*" *Amen* is much more than a period. It is a word of praise and acclamation that can add power to the simplest prayer, or be used alone to praise God.

Hosanna could be translated "Grant salvation!" and was used by the Jewish people as a prayer of praise during the Feast of Booths (Leviticus 23:33–43). At that feast, they waved tree branches, rejoiced, and shouted "Hosanna." The people of Jerusalem saw this as an appropriate way to welcome Jesus on what is now observed as Palm Sunday. Hosanna is used as an acclamation of praise in the "Holy, holy, holy," that serves as our response to the preface at Mass.

PRAISING THE GOD OF CREATION

In Chapter One we discussed how modern scientists have discovered incredible facts about the vastness of the universe and the complexity of creation. These facts have led many former atheists to find and adore God as a mighty creator. All the works of creation should encourage us to worship and adore God. And we don't need an expensive telescope or electron microscope. God is present in all the beauties of nature.

But we must open our eyes. "Ever since the creation of the world his eternal power and divine nature, invisible though they are, have been understood and seen through the things he has made" (Romans 1:20). If we refuse to look beyond the visible, we become like those who pluck blackberries but miss the God who made them.

I've always admired those with eyes open to beauty and the flame of God's presence. Rob, a good friend and expert fly fisherman, is fond of saying that he goes to the mountains to fly fish and talk to God. When I asked him about this, he responded:

I am refreshed emotionally and spiritually when I go fishing. Trout streams are always in the most interesting places. There is such beauty in landscapes. Streams mesmerize me. Wildlife is nearby in some form or another. The early morning and late evening light, rain and snow storms, cloudy and sunny days, hold a certain magic. I suspect it goes to my very roots as a human being that I see God in all these things, even the gentle whisper of a breeze (1 Kings 19:9–13). Nature shows the perfection of our Creator. Everything works in perfect harmony. There is balance and efficiency, along with a capacity to change and adapt as the need arises. All I have to do is be aware. God can be discovered in everything created.

Whether we fish, hike, or garden, we find reason to worship. Daniel 3:57ff is a canticle that invites us to join all creation in praising God: "Bless the Lord, all you works of the Lord." Life has so much more to offer than what meets the eye. When we see a bush aflame with berries, we certainly ought to enjoy them (perhaps smearing our faces with blackberry juice), but we also should worship the God who made them.

That expression, "Bless the Lord," is found often in Scripture and deserves special mention. The word *bless* may mean to ask God to show favor to someone as in the expression, "God bless you." Or it may mean to honor as holy, as when we "bless the Lord." There are many Old Testament blessing prayers that praise God. A good example is Psalm 103, whose first verse is an enthusiastic invitation to glorify God: "Bless the LORD, O my soul, / and all that is within me, / bless his holy name." Many New Testament prayers bless God. The canticle of Zechariah sings: "Blessed be the Lord God of Israel, / for he has looked favorably on his people and redeemed them" (Luke 1:68). Saint Paul often blesses God in his letters, praising God for favoring us: "Blessed be the God and Father of our Lord Jesus Christ, who has blessed us in Christ with every spiritual blessing in the heavenly places" (Ephesians 1:3).

ADORATION AND
RESPECT FOR CREATION

I remember seeing a cartoon where a monk was standing on a hill watching a beautiful sunset. As he watched the sun disappear in the west, he raised his eyes to heaven and shouted, "Encore! Encore!"

Appreciation of the beauty of creation and respect for God's creative power are aspects of adoration that should be a part of our relationship to God. The *Catechism of the Catholic Church* states:

> *Each creature possesses its own particular goodness and perfection.* For each one of the works of the "six days" it is said: "And God saw that it was good." "By the very nature of creation, material being is endowed with its own stability, truth, and excellence, its own order and laws." Each of the various creatures, willed in its own being, reflects in its own way a ray of God's infinite wisdom and goodness. Man must therefore respect the particular goodness of every creature, to avoid any disordered use of things which would be in contempt of the Creator and would bring disastrous consequences for human beings and their environment (339).

The *Catechism*, in a poetically beautiful passage, points out the connection between creation and worship. God created the earth—the visible, material world. The Book of Genesis symbolically presents creation as a succession of six days of divine work to teach us basic truths about the created order. All things owe their existence to God. Every creature is good, and we must respect this goodness. The beauty of the universe comes from the diversity of created beings and the relationships among them, with humanity as the summit of the Creator's work. All creatures are ordered to God's glory. This glory is expressed in the Sabbath rest, which reminds us that we must orient ourselves and all creation to God, especially in worship (CCC 337–354).

It is noteworthy that even some secular writers are coming to appreciate how reverence for God and respect for God's creation are important to the betterment of our world. Environmentalist Bill McKibben wrote that one of the most important possibilities of taking care of our planet is...

a new link with communities of faith in this country. Though they don't always live up to their ideals, churches and synagogues and mosques are among the few institutions that can posit some idea for human existence other than accumulation....[Religious groups affirm] "This is God's world," ...which is a shocking idea for a culture that's come to think of everything as ours. It's precisely this ability of religious leaders of all stripes to see individuals as part of something larger than ourselves that's so important (*National Geographic*, August 2006).

God does know what is best for us. When we bow down before God in adoration, joyfully affirming the beauty of creation, we not only worship God. We also help make this world what it ought to be. We begin to realize the privilege of being made in God's image and likeness so that we might exercise dominion over the earth and help make it the beautiful garden of plenty God intended from the beginning (Genesis 1:27–31).

ACTS OF FAITH, HOPE, AND LOVE

The Catholic Church assigns special importance to the virtues of faith, hope, and love. They are called *theological virtues* because they are gifts of God and direct our relationship to God. By *faith* we believe in God and accept the truths that God reveals. By *hope* we desire heaven as our final goal and have confident assurance of achieving it with the help of God's grace. By *love* we cherish God above all, and our neighbor as ourselves.

We adore God when we profess our faith, hope, and love. Faith acclaims God as the supreme being. Hope acknowledges God as our final destiny. Love expresses our readiness to accept the gift of love from God and share it with others. Scripture offers model prayers of faith (Mark 9:24), hope (Luke 23:42), and love (John 21:17). Catholic prayer books offer patterns for such prayers. And, taught by Scripture and tradition, we may offer these prayers of adoration in our own words.

All our attitudes of praise and adoration may be expressed in a prayer said frequently by many Catholics. "Glory to the Father, and to the Son, and to the Holy Spirit. As it was in the beginning, is now and ever shall be, world without end. Amen."

CONTRITION

Adoration leads to contrition. God's greatness, expressed in the vast beauty of creation, God's incredible love, shared in the life, death, and resurrection of Jesus, and God's awesome wisdom, seen in the outpouring of the Holy Spirit, should leave us amazed. Scripture tells us that we are created in the image and likeness of God (Genesis 1:26), and that we are children of God (Romans 8:16). Jesus directs us to be perfect as our heavenly Father is perfect (Matthew 5:48). All this is reason for adoration and praise.

But who could live up to such a noble calling? Only the

Mother of Jesus. She was addressed by the angel Gabriel as full
of grace. The rest of us fall short of the mark. We sin. We offend
God. Once we become aware of who God is and of who we are,
the only appropriate response is contrition, sorrow for sin.

If we offend a good friend, we are quick to apologize. We've
all had the experience of causing pain to someone we love, asking
pardon, and receiving forgiveness. Apologies, sincerely given and
accepted, can strengthen a friendship and turn hurt to happiness.
This is true in our relationship with God. God's compassion
turns the sorrow of our sinfulness into the joy of being forgiven.
"Happy are those whose transgression is forgiven, / whose sin is
covered" (Psalm 32:1).

Scripture teaches us how to ask forgiveness. Psalm 51, David's
act of sorrow, expresses grief for human weakness and begs
God's forgiveness. The humble prayer of a tax collector, "God,
be merciful to me, a sinner!" (Luke 18:13), is an excellent act
of contrition. In the Lord's Prayer, we ask for forgiveness and
are reminded to forgive others: "Forgive us our trespasses as we
forgive those who trespass against us."

Jesus left his Church a sign of God's forgiveness, the sacrament of penance. Here we are privileged to meet Jesus, confess
our sins, and hear him assure us of pardon. In connection with
the sacrament of penance, the Church offers several prayers that
may be used as an Act of Contrition. We may also express sorrow in our own words.

Jesus brings a richer and deeper meaning to our understanding
of contrition when he tells us, "Blessed are the poor in spirit, for
theirs is the kingdom of heaven" (Matthew 5:3). The poor in spirit
are those who know they can claim nothing as their own except
their weakness and sin. They recognize their utter dependence
on God, and find security in the knowledge that their lives are in
God's hands. On the cross, Jesus completely submitted his human
life to God: "Father, into your hands I commend my spirit" (Luke
23:46). The criminal crucified with Jesus knew that he himself

had been reduced to utter poverty. Poor in spirit, he put his trust in Jesus and was rewarded with the kingdom of heaven.

Today's world denies the reality of sin, and we can easily underestimate the awfulness of even the slightest offense against God. An adequate treatment of these issues is impossible in a book of this size. For a more thorough explanation of sin and sorrow, Chapter Ten, "Reconciliation—Jesus Forgives" in *"We Believe..." A Survey of the Catholic Faith* (see bibliography) provides a Bible-based explanation of sin and repentance, as well as an examination of conscience based on the Ten Commandments as explained in the *Catechism of the Catholic Church.*

THANKSGIVING

If you've ever sent a gift to a friend or relative without receiving a thank-you note or a phone call acknowledging the gift, you've probably felt hurt or unappreciated. We might suppose that this is why we should express thanks to God. If we don't, God is likely to be offended or upset.

Nothing could be further from the truth. God does not need our gratitude, nor is God upset by our ingratitude. Scripture bids us to "give thanks in all circumstances; for this is the will of God in Christ Jesus for you" (1 Thessalonians 5:18). But this is not to benefit God. It is to benefit us. As Preface IV for Weekdays proclaims:

> *Father, all-powerful and ever-living God,*
> *we do well always and everywhere to give you thanks.*
>
> *You have no need of our praise,*
> *yet our desire to thank you is itself your gift.*
> *Our prayer of thanksgiving adds nothing*
> *to your greatness,*
> *but makes us grow in your grace,*
> *through Jesus Christ our Lord.*

Gratitude is important because it connects us to the Source of all good gifts. We are quick to thank friends for favors. Recognizing the gifts we receive from others and appreciating their generosity brings us closer to them. When we take time to count God's blessings and offer thanks, we move closer to the loving heart of God. "O give thanks to the LORD, for he is good, / for his steadfast love endures forever" (Psalm 136:1).

GRATITUDE IS GOOD FOR US

Father Stephen Rossetti, in a recent book, mentions the research of psychologists Michael McCullough, PhD, and Robert Emmons, PhD. Their studies show that people who worked at being grateful were better off physically, psychologically, and spiritually. He continues:

> Physically, the gratitude group exercised more, had fewer physical symptoms, and slept better. Psychologically, they reported higher levels of alertness, enthusiasm, determination, and energy. They experienced less depression and stress as well as high levels of optimism and life satisfaction, without denying the negative aspects of their lives. Spiritually, they were more likely to help others, they were less envious of others, less materialistic, more generous, and more likely to attend religious services and engage in religious activities. Clearly, being grateful is good for you (*The Joy of Priesthood*, pp. 156–157).

PRAYERS OF THANKS

The greatest prayer of thanks is the Eucharist (*eucharist* means "giving thanks"), and we will study the Mass in Chapter Six. There are many hymns of thanks in the Old Testament. Psalm 100 emphasizes the happiness brought to us by God, who calls us his own:

Make a joyful noise to the LORD, all the earth.
Worship the LORD with gladness;
come into his presence with singing.

Know that the LORD is God.
It is he that made us, and we are his;
we are his people, and the sheep of his pasture.

Enter his gates with thanksgiving,
and his courts with praise.
Give thanks to him, bless his name.

For the LORD is good;
his steadfast love endures forever,
and his faithfulness to all generations.

The gospels show that Jesus offered frequent prayers of thanksgiving (Matthew 11:25, John 11:41). He thanked God at meals (Matthew 13:56) and above all at the Last Supper, his Eucharist (Luke 22:17). In imitation of Jesus, we should always offer thanks to God before and after meals.

Sometimes we forget or look for excuses not to pray at meals. I read about a family that sat down to supper one evening. The mother asked, "Whose turn is it to say grace tonight?" "Mine," said the teenage daughter, "but I really don't think we have to pray over leftovers. We've already said grace for this meal three times."

We need not look for excuses to avoid prayers of thanks, contrition, or adoration. It is worth noting that while we may not get exactly what we ask for in prayers of petition (more about this in the next chapter), prayers of adoration, contrition, and thanks are always heard the way we desire. They are prayers that never fail!

BURNING BUSHES, FAITH, AND PRAYER

The young parents whose unborn daughter was endangered by serious heart defects wanted to know how to pray. I made several simple suggestions. This was not a time for a complicated theology of prayer.

But the situation did call for adoration, contrition, thanks, and petition, perhaps a prayer like this: "Dear God, the life of our child is in your hands. We believe you are a loving Father, and that you care for us. We have not always prayed to you as we should, but we humbly turn to you now, trusting in your mercy. We thank you for the gift of our child's life and we ask you to keep her from all harm. Send your Holy Spirit to guide the doctors who will be caring for her. Help us face the future with courage, knowing that Jesus, our Good Shepherd, is at our side in every dark valley, guiding us to the light of your love. Amen."

When the little girl was born, she faced grave challenges. Her parents named her "Faith" and had her baptized immediately. She has had the three required surgeries. All have gone well. For five years we celebrated her birthday with a Mass of thanksgiving. She is now six years old, a smiling bundle of energy and love.

Six years ago, Faith's parents found themselves before a burning bush not of their own choosing. Like Moses, they saw the Lord. There are times when we too stand before a burning bush. May we see the Lord, and take off our shoes in acts of adoration, contrition, thanksgiving, and petition.

QUESTIONS FOR
DISCUSSION AND REFLECTION

What is your favorite prayer? How do you remember to offer prayers of adoration, contrition, and thanks as well as prayers of petition?

There is an old saying, "On the highway of life, prayer should be your steering wheel, not your spare tire." What do you think this means? How can you make it more applicable in your life?

While it is true that prayer should be our steering wheel, not just our spare tire, God is always available in emergencies. In fact, God has a 911 number. It is Psalm 91, verse 1 (and 2):

> *You who live in the shelter of the Most High,*
> *who abide in the shadow of the Almighty,*
> *will say to the LORD, "My refuge and my fortress;*
> *my God, in whom I trust."*

Is this a prayer of supplication, or adoration, or both?

Read this "Internet gem" and consider how it relates to Elizabeth Barrett Browning's verse that begins this chapter. *The man whispered, "God, speak to me" and a meadowlark sang. But the man did not hear. So the man shouted, "God speak to me!" and the thunder rolled across the sky. But the man did not listen. The man looked around and said, "God let me see you," and a star shone brightly. But the man did not notice. The man begged, "God show me a miracle" and a child was born. But the man did not understand. So, the man cried out in despair, "Touch me God and let me know that you are here!" Whereupon God reached down and touched the man. But the man brushed the butterfly away and walked on.*

ACTIVITIES

In this chapter we have used the traditional division of prayer as adoration, contrition, thanksgiving, and supplication. The *Catechism of the Catholic Church* offers a more complex division of prayer. Study this summary of sections 2623 to 2649 from the *Catechism* and fit these categories into the four we've just studied.

In prayers of *blessing and adoration,* God blesses us in Christ with the grace of the Spirit, and we bless God, adoring God as Supreme Being, as Creator, Redeemer, and Spirit of Love. *Petition* expresses our dependence on God and asks God for forgiveness, for the coming of God's kingdom, and for other spiritual and material needs. Prayer of *intercession* imitates the prayer of Jesus for others. *Thanksgiving,* expressed especially in the Eucharist, communicates our gratitude to God for every good gift. *Praise* recognizes that God *is* God, declaring our joyful wonder at God's goodness and greatness.

Chapter Four

SUPPLICATION:
ASK, AND IT WILL
BE GIVEN YOU

❧

When I was in fourth grade, I wanted a bicycle so I could get a job delivering newspapers. But I couldn't afford a bicycle without a job, and couldn't get a job without a bicycle. Religion class at our Catholic school seemed to offer a solution. We studied prayer, and reflected on Jesus' promise, "Ask, and it will be given you" (Matthew 7:7). We considered other reassuring passages. "I will do whatever you ask in my name" (John 14:13). "So I tell you, whatever you ask for in prayer, believe that you have received it, and it will be yours" (Mark 11:24). To make things even better, a store in town was raffling off a bicycle as a promotion. Tickets were free. You just had to sign your name and address. I did that and immediately started praying to win the raffle. I was absolutely certain I would because Jesus had promised, "Ask, and it will be given you." I was so confident, in fact, that I told my younger brother I knew I'd win the bike. When he expressed skepticism, I challenged him to a five dollar bet. He was so overwhelmed by my confidence that he wouldn't take the bet, which was just as well since neither of us had five dollars!

The raffle was held. I did *not* win the bike. I'm not sure how my fourth-grade theology withstood this test of my faith, but I think someone pointed out that many other children wanted that

same bicycle. If God pulled my ticket, it wouldn't be fair to all
the others who were also praying to win.

FROM RAFFLES TO THE REAL WORLD

I soon discovered that there were other ways of getting a bicycle,
like mowing lawns and saving money. And while a new bike is
a big deal to a fourth-grader, it is trivial compared to the real
challenges and tragedies faced by people every day.

A young mother of two small children is diagnosed with cancer. She and her family, her parish, and thousands of others pray
for her healing. She is treated by the best doctors, and at times
seems to make progress. But as months of suffering and treatment
drag on, the cancer grows worse. She dies in her early thirties,
leaving behind a grieving husband and two small children. She
is mourned by a loving family and many friends. They entrust
her soul to God, but wonder why their prayers for her healing
were not answered.

Jesus teaches us to ask for what we need—prayer of supplication. But what about petitions that are not granted as we'd like?
What do we do when we feel God hasn't heard our prayers? There
are no easy answers. Nevertheless, we must look at the questions.

And the questions become even more difficult when we
consider human tragedy at its worst, like the wickedness of the
Nazi regime during the Second World War. Elie Wiesel, in his
book, *Night,* describes the unrelenting horrors of the Nazi death
camps. Arrested with his parents and three sisters in 1944 and
brought to Auschwitz when he was fifteen years old, Elie saw
his mother and youngest sister hauled away to the gas chamber
and crematorium. He and his father were forced to work at hard
labor under appalling conditions. They were marched to Buchenwald in the dead of winter, and Elie's father died of starvation
and exhaustion just a few months before the camp was liberated.
Elie had seen outrages beyond imagining: babies tossed into the

air and used for target practice by German troops, woman and children pushed alive into trenches filled with blazing gasoline, cruelties without number. This young lad, a devout Jew, could not understand why his prayers went unheard. He could only wonder how God could be found in the unspeakable misery of the death camps.

While we have not faced death, as Elie did at Auschwitz and Buchenwald, we know of the atrocities that took place there. We must ask the questions Elie asked: How can God allow such evil? Why does God not intervene? Where is God at such times? Is there a God?

DOES GOD EXIST?

It is possible to pray acts of adoration, contrition, and thanksgiving, and never doubt God's existence. But when we petition God for things that seem right, when a family asks for healing of a young mother stricken with cancer, when inmates of death camps pray for mercy...and silence is the only answer, questions arise. Is there a God? What reasons do I have for belief?

After forty years in the priesthood, I'm more convinced than ever that God exists. My reasons are these: "Everything cannot come from nothing. Organization cannot happen by chance. Belief in God makes us the best we can be." These reasons are developed in my books, *"We Believe..." A Survey of the Catholic Faith* (Chapter One) and *The Search for Happiness* (Chapter Four).

But I don't depend only on my own experience and reasoning. I've been strongly influenced by former atheists who have come to the conclusion (usually against their own inclinations and intellectual formation) that God indeed exists. I've read the works of such former atheists, intellectuals like C. S. Lewis (*Mere Christianity, Surprised by Joy*), astronomers like Dr. Allan Sandage (*Newsweek*, July 20, 1998), physicians like Dr. Diane

Komp (*Images of Grace*), Dr. Larry Dossey (*Healing Words*), and
Nobel Prize winner Dr. Alexis Carrel (*The Voyage to Lourdes*),
educators like Mortimer Adler (*How to Think About God*),
journalists like André Frossard (*I Have Met Him: God Exists*),
and philosophers like Dr. Antony Flew.

God is not "pie in the sky," the wishful thinking of dreamers.
God is so real that those who have had every reason to deny God's
existence find themselves drawn to belief despite all obstacles. Elie
Wiesel described his spiritual state as he stood in the death camp,
desolated by the loss of everything: "I was the accuser, God the
accused. My eyes had opened and I was alone, terribly alone in
a world without God, without man" (*Night*, by Elie Wiesel, page
68). Yet, forty years later, Elie could say at his Nobel Peace Prize
acceptance speech in Oslo on December 10, 1986: "Blessed be
Thou...for giving us life, for sustaining us, and for enabling us
to reach this day....I have faith. Faith in the God of Abraham,
Isaac, and Jacob, and even in His creation. Without it no action
would be possible" (*Night*, pp. 117, 120).

Elie did not find God in the death camps, but the God of
Abraham was there, a co-sufferer in the person of his Son, Jesus
Christ. "For God so loved the world that he gave his only Son, so
that everyone who believes in him may not perish but may have
eternal life" (John 3:16). François Mauriac, a renowned Catholic
author and the 1952 Nobel Laureate in Literature, befriended
Elie after the war and convinced him to write about his experiences. In his foreword to *Night,* Mauriac asked in regard to his
young friend:

> Did I speak to him of that other Jew, this crucified brother
> who perhaps resembled him and whose cross conquered
> the world? Did I explain to him that what had been a
> stumbling block for *his* faith had become a cornerstone
> for *mine*? And that the connection between the cross
> and human suffering remains, in my view, the key to the

unfathomable mystery in which the faith of his childhood
was lost? (*Night*, p. xxi)

We dare to look at life with all its sorrows and mysteries. We
are neither foolish nor naive when we believe in God in the worst
of times, even when our prayers seem unanswered and God seems
silent. For we follow a Master who used his divine power not to
crush evil, but to absorb it into his own body on the cross, and
by his suffering and death to destroy death. It was not easy for
Jesus. He took upon himself all the physical pain and shattered
emotions of those who would ever feel abandoned by God. From
the cross he cried out, "My God, my God, why have you forsaken
me?" (Matthew 27:46). Then he brought all the desolation of
humanity, the pain of Job, and the loneliness of Elie Wiesel, to
the heart of a loving God. "Father, into your hands I commend
my spirit" (Luke 23:46).

WHY SUFFERING AND DEATH?

But why must there be suffering and death? The answers to this
question are not easy, but they are linked to human freedom. God
is love, and God created human beings to enjoy the happiness
that comes from loving and being loved. This requires freedom
because love cannot be forced. If we are free to love, we must
also be free to refuse love. Sadly, Adam and Eve refused love and
said no to God. Like them, we can misuse the gift of freedom by
disobeying God. In so doing, we hurt ourselves and others. God
allows this because otherwise we could not be free.

Perhaps we can see how God must allow people to harm
others if freedom is to be real. But what about evils that seem
to come from nature, like cancer? Again, the answer is freedom.
God gave wonderful abilities so we could do our part to bring
this world to perfection. We might suppose that the world would
be better if it were already perfect, but God knows that while we

live in time, we need to make a contribution. A world existing in time must be a world in process. Time allows the satisfaction of achievement and the rewards of helping others.

But down through the ages, people have used their talents for evil purposes as well as for good. Some individuals have campaigned against God's commandments and providential plan for us. As a result, awful wars and terrible evils have devastated our world. Immense possibilities for good have been left untouched. Most of the tragedies that darken our days could long ago have been eliminated if we had obeyed God's commandments. Every disease could have been conquered. Harmony with nature—including nature's energies of fire, wind, water, and motion—could have been achieved. Our world could have been, as God intended, a natural transition to the eternal happiness that is our ultimate destiny.

But through countless ages humanity has repeated the refusal of Adam and Eve to obey. So we live in a world far short of what it should be. Disease, tragedy, grief, and the uncertainties of death trouble us and erode our efforts to find happiness. God could have remedied this situation by simply annihilating us. But for reasons we may never fully comprehend, God entered our world. Jesus took upon himself the suffering of humanity. He carried the cross to forever unite himself to our pain. He died on that cross and rose in order to lead us through death to eternal joy. (For an expanded discussion of these issues, see *The Search for Happiness*, Chapter Five.)

TO PRAY IN JESUS' NAME

Trusting, then, in God who suffers with us, we reflect on the promises of Jesus. On the night before he died, he said, "Very truly, I tell you, if you ask anything of the Father in my name, he will give it to you" (John 16:23). Catholics believe that any passage in Scripture must be considered in the light of the whole

Bible. Other promises of Jesus, such as, "Ask, and it will be given you" (Matthew 7:7), and "So I tell you, whatever you ask for in prayer, believe that you have received it, and it will be yours" (Mark 11:24) must not be taken in isolation, but in the context of John 16:23. Christians must always pray in Jesus' name. This means we pray as Jesus did.

The same night Jesus promised, "If you ask anything of the Father in my name, he will give it to you," he himself prayed to the Father. He knelt in the Garden of Gethsemane and said, "Father, if you are willing, remove this cup from me; yet, not my will but yours be done" (Luke 22:42). He prayed with complete submission to the Father's will. That is what it means to pray in Jesus' name.

What Jesus wanted in his anguish was to be relieved of the cup of suffering. But instead, "an angel from heaven appeared to him and gave him strength" (Luke 22:43). In the Lord's Prayer, Jesus taught us to say, "Thy will be done." Prayer in Jesus' name does not seek to bring God around to our way of thinking but to bring us around to God's way of thinking. God's way of thinking may not be ours. We may pray that God will take away pain or disability and receive instead the patience and strength to endure, as Saint Paul did (2 Corinthians 12:7–9).

This kind of prayer gives ordinary human beings the power to bring God's light and grace into the darkest night of suffering. Saint Maximilian Kolbe, a Franciscan priest, was arrested in 1941 by the German Gestapo for harboring Jewish refugees and speaking out against Nazism. He was condemned to Auschwitz as a slave laborer. He was Christ to other prisoners, sharing his bread, hearing confessions, encouraging the disheartened with prayer and meditations on the passion of Jesus. When a prisoner disappeared, the Nazis chose ten men at random to die as a deterrent to escape attempts. One of the ten selected to die, Franciszek Gajowniczek, began to cry: "My wife! My children! I will never see them again!" At this, Maximilian stepped forward and asked to die in his place. His request was granted, and along with nine others he was thrown into a bunker to starve. One by one, the prisoners died of hunger and thirst. After two weeks, only four were alive and the bunker was needed for more victims. The camp executioner gave a lethal injection to the four dying men. Father Kolbe, the only one still fully conscious, gave his arm for the injection with a prayer on his lips. Franciszek Gajowniczek survived the camps, attended Father Kolbe's canonization in 1982, and until his own death in 1995 paid homage to the saint who had brought Christ's love where there had been only hate and despair.

Prayer in Jesus' name, with submission to the Father's will, has its greatest power in places that stretch love to the limit, places like Gethsemane and Auschwitz. But it is required of us all. We must all face death some day. We must all pray for things great and small with submission to God's will, with trust in God's providence.

Doctor Robert retired from medicine after many years of service to others. He moved to Montana to be closer to his family, to fish with his son and play with his grandchildren. But he was soon diagnosed with terminal cancer. When I expressed my sympathy at this, he said, "God doesn't owe me anything. I've had more blessings than I can ever repay. I'd like a few more years, but whatever God wishes is fine. I only want what God wants."

FORGIVE US AS WE FORGIVE

Jesus taught us to pray, "Forgive us our trespasses as we forgive those who trespass against us." In his Sermon on the Mount he explained, "For if you forgive others their trespasses, your heavenly Father will also forgive you; but if you do not forgive others, neither will your Father forgive your trespasses" (Matthew 6:14–15). Prayer cannot be separated into compartments, so forgiveness of others is essential if we expect any petition to be heard by God. Praying in Jesus' name, then, implies forgiveness of others in imitation of our Lord.

And just as praying with submission to God's will can apply to anything from bicycles to Buchenwald, so forgiveness of others can cover a vast territory. It is easy for us to resent slights from others, or the foibles and faults of family members. We harbor grudges and carry burdens of resentment. We refuse to forgive small things, then place petitions before God, expecting to be granted a favorable hearing. But carrying grudges and failing to forgive can isolate us from God in matters small or serious. It has been noted that a bird can be held down by a slender thread or a massive chain. It matters not which, as long as either is unbroken. So too, we can tie ourselves off from the mercy of God because of resentments slight or serious. It matters not, as long as the bond is unbroken.

So how can we forgive others and open ourselves to God's bounty? We should meditate on Jesus parable of the unforgiving servant, which teaches that offenses against ourselves are insignificant compared to any offense against God (Matthew 18:23–35). We should reflect on the example of Jesus, who forgave his enemies from the cross: "Father, forgive them; for they do not know what they are doing" (Luke 23:34). And when we find ourselves harboring petty grudges and counting off reasons why some offender does not deserve pardon, we must look to the example of believers who had every reason to hate, but instead freely forgave.

J. Neville Ward's book, *Five for Sorrow, Ten for Joy*, presents an extraordinary example of forgiveness, a prayer found written on a piece of wrapping paper in Ravensbrück, a Nazi concentration camp for women, when it was liberated:

O Lord, remember not only the men and women of good will, but also those of ill will. But do not remember all the suffering they have inflicted on us. Remember the fruits we brought, thanks to this suffering: our comradeship, our loyalty, our humility, the courage, the generosity, the greatness of heart which has grown out of this; and when they come to judgment, let all the fruits that we have borne be their forgiveness (p. 63).

We cannot read this prayer without being encouraged to forgive the failings of others. That victim in Ravensbrück cast off iron chains that might keep her outside the boundaries of God's mercy. How can we not cut the slender thread of hurt that keeps us from openness to God's gracious gifts? If we want to pray with Jesus, in his name, we must pray with submission to the Father's will. We must forgive others as we wish to be forgiven.

Closely related to the issue of forgiveness is the fact that God may not answer some prayers because we build up walls between ourselves and the Lord. We sever communications with God by sin, whereas we open ourselves up to God's blessings by holiness of life. "Beloved, if our hearts do not condemn us, we have boldness before God; and we receive from him whatever we ask, because we obey his commandments and do what pleases him" (1 John 3:21–22).

FOR WHAT MAY WE PRAY?

I've often been asked if it is permissible to pray for ourselves, not only for spiritual blessings, but for material ones as well. One reading of the psalms indicates we may ask God for anything that is good. The New Testament contains many prayers for spiritual blessings, like Paul's prayer in Ephesians 3:14–21. And the Mother of Jesus shows us that material cares, no matter how small, may be placed before the Lord. At the wedding feast of Cana, she noticed that the wine had run out. To save their hosts from embarrassment, she brought this to the attention of Jesus. He promptly changed water into wine to keep the party going.

We pray, then, in Jesus' name, for good things, spiritual and material. We pray with submission to the Father's will, having forgiven our enemies. Will we always get exactly what we ask for, when we want it? No, for many reasons. We will examine some of those reasons now.

GOD'S TIME AND OURS

When we ask for something in Jesus' name, we must consider the difference between God's time and ours. Someone has remarked, "God has forever, and sometimes likes to take it!" Time is relative. The days before Christmas seem to drag on interminably for little children, while years rush by too quickly for the elderly. God exists in eternity, where there is no past or future. God does have forever, and God may take more time than we'd like to respond to our requests. Jesus, in his humorous parables about the insistent friend (Luke 11:5–8) and the widow who kept seeking justice from an unjust judge (Luke 18:1–7), teaches the importance of perseverance when we pray. When we ask for anything, we must persevere in prayer and wait for an answer in God's time.

Many years ago a married couple came to me with real problems. The husband showed his love for his wife and children by working hard and providing a good living. The wife, however, wanted her husband to be more attentive to her emotional needs. Eventually, she became involved in an affair with a man who seemed to be a good listener. When her husband discovered this, he asked what was wrong. She explained her feelings, and he said he would do anything to preserve their marriage. He truly loved his wife and children. When they came to see me, the wife agreed that her husband had become everything she had ever wanted. This should have ended the affair and restored family unity. But although he had become the ideal husband, it wasn't enough. "All those years," she shouted, "I prayed that my husband would understand my feelings. Now it's happened, but only after I've fallen in love with someone else. It's too late! It's too late!" She left her husband and children for the other man, who walked away from the relationship a short time later. The situation became a tragedy because she wanted her prayers heard on her time frame, not God's.

Like her, we can be impatient with God. Perseverance in prayer can seem too difficult a burden. But we must try to see things from God's point of view. One way of getting perspective on God's time is to see our lives in contrast with the time since the beginning of creation. We may live one hundred years. The universe began fourteen billion years ago! Scientists have suggested that to gain some perspective on the relationship of our life span to the time since creation is to condense the fourteen billion years into one. Creation occurs on January 1. The Earth is formed on September 14. Dinosaurs begin to prowl the planet on December 24. The first humans appear on December 31 at 10:30 PM. Jesus was born four seconds ago. The longest human life is one fifth of a second. This is God's time, and this is how we will see our lives on Earth from the vantage point of eternity.

I suspect that from eternity we shall see the patient suffering of Saint Maximilian Kolbe in a new light. We shall see that even a lifetime of waiting for an answer to prayer was only a moment. So when we place our petitions before God, we must be willing to wait on the Lord, to be "imitators of those who through faith and patience inherit the promises" (Hebrews 6:12).

Spiritual Needs and Material Wants

While the Bible teaches us to pray for both spiritual and material needs, we can pray with more assurance for spiritual blessings than for material benefits. Jesus says, "If you then, who are evil, know how to give good gifts to your children, how much more will the heavenly Father give the Holy Spirit to those who ask him!" (Luke 11:13). We may pray for prosperity, but such a prayer might merit a positive answer less than a prayer for humility.

Further, there are complications in praying for material blessings. Farmers and gardeners pray for the rain needed by their crops, while children want sunny weather for their Little League championship game. It's easy to see my own requests as matters involving just God and me. But God must fit my prayers into a pattern that includes all the plans and desires of six billion other people. Our world is like a giant jigsaw puzzle of six billion living pieces constantly changing shape and location. This living puzzle has been in the process of formation for hundreds of thousands of years and will not be completed until the end of time. Only God can fit my prayer into such a pattern. I cannot. I must pray and trust in God's providence.

And in praying for material needs we can sometimes ask for the wrong things. The apostles James and John did exactly this when they requested special places close to Jesus (Mark 10:35–45). As Jesus pointed out, they did not know what they were asking. Like them, we can seek favors from God that seem good to us, but might actually be hurtful to ourselves or others.

One of my favorite stories illustrates how it's easy to ask for the wrong things. Father Murphy was making visitations of every home in the parish. As he chatted with Mrs. O'Brien, he noticed that she had a parrot in her living room. He walked over to the cage, and the parrot eyed him, sashayed over, and squawked, "Hi, there. I'm Gertie. And I'm a swinger!" "Mrs. O'Brien," gasped the pastor, "that bird will give scandal to everyone who comes to this home!" "I'm sorry," said Mrs. O'Brien, "but I bought Gertie from a sailor, and she's always talked like that. I can't do anything with her." "Tell you what," said Father Murphy, "I like parrots and have two of them back at the rectory. But they're Christian birds. They don't do a thing all day but pray the rosary. I'll take Gertie back to the rectory and put her with my parrots, and they'll reform her." "Well," said Mrs. O'Brien, "if you think that might help, go ahead." So Father Murphy covered Gertie's cage and hauled her over to the rectory. Sure enough, there were his two parrots in their cage, praying the rosary. He took Gertie out and placed her in their cage. She blinked once or twice, then squawked, "Hi, there. I'm Gertie. And I'm a swinger!" The two parrots looked at each other for a moment, then one said to the other: "Put away those beads, Charlie. Our prayers have been answered!"

Whatever it takes to remind us that God knows best! James and John in Scripture and a parrot story, the sublime and the ridiculous, both can remind us how God's wisdom far surpasses our wishes and how God's providence is preferable to our own plans. There have been times in my life when I asked God for something, certain that it was best. When my request wasn't granted, I was disappointed. But from that "unanswered prayer" came rich blessings far beyond what I could have imagined. God knows best, yet another reason to pray, "Thy will be done."

Praying With Faith

Jesus said, "So I tell you, whatever you ask for in prayer, believe that you have received it, and it will be yours" (Mark 11:24). There are Christians who suppose this means we will always receive exactly what we want if only we have enough faith. They suppose if we do not receive what we request, it is because we lack faith. Many years ago I was making hospital visits and stopped at a room in the cancer ward. The woman in the room was crying, and I asked if she wanted to talk. "Yes," she said. "My friend just came for a visit. She told me that if I prayed with faith I would be healed. I'm not being healed. I'm dying. This must mean I don't have faith, and can't go to heaven."

I pointed out to her that Jesus' words in Mark 11:24 must be taken in the context of the whole Bible, of Jesus' own prayer in Gethsemane, and of Paul's prayer for healing from his "thorn in the flesh" (see 2 Corinthians 12:7–9). When Paul asked to be delivered, he received instead the reply, "My grace is sufficient for you, for power is made perfect in weakness." Another time, when Paul prayed for the healing of a fellow missionary, he was not heard as he hoped. He reports, "Trophimus I left ill in Miletus" (2 Timothy 4:20). Did Paul not have sufficient faith? Of course he did. Praying with faith means praying with submission to God's will.

Dr. Larry Dossey is a retired surgeon, a former chief of staff at Humana Medical Center in Dallas. He was an unbeliever until he studied experiments showing how prayer helps bring about healing. Convinced by his study, he now is a firm believer in God, in the immortality of the human soul, and in the power of prayer. In his book, *Healing Words: The Power of Prayer and the Practice of Medicine*, he remarks that the power of prayer is so evident that doctors who don't pray for their patients may soon be accused of malpractice!

But why doesn't prayer for healing always work? Dr. Dossey says that as a physician he would dearly love to have a prayer that never failed when his patients needed it. But if all prayers for recovery were uniformly answered, no one would die and the earth would quickly become overpopulated, and no one would go to heaven. This proves, Dr. Dossey asserts, that we are not wise enough to use a prayer that always works. The best prayer is the one Jesus teaches, "Thy will be done." We pray for healing for ourselves or for others, but we leave the final answer to the infinite wisdom and loving providence of God.

There's a humorous story that illustrates how we don't always understand the possible consequences of our requests. A man walking on a beach noticed a lamp. He picked it up and brushed off the sand. Out came a genie who said: "Thank you for releasing me. I will grant you three wishes." "First," the man said, "I'd like one billion dollars." Poof. A certificate appeared in the man's hand giving him access to a Swiss bank account for one billion dollars. "Second, I'd like a red Ferrari convertible." Poof. There it was, with the keys on the front seat. "Third, I'd like to be irresistible to women." Poof. The genie turned him into a box of chocolates.

There are other issues related to faith that should be considered. On one hand, it is a mistake to blame ourselves for lack of faith every time a petition seems to go unanswered. On the other hand, it is probably a mistake to assume that our faith is all it should be. Perhaps our prayers might be more effective if our faith were stronger. Without worrying, we should ask God for the grace of faith, then pray, entrusting the answer to God.

Finally, we may lack confidence, not because God fails to answer our prayers, but because we do not recognize God's answers. We are given what we ask, then wonder if it wasn't just a coincidence. (Someone has observed: "Coincidences happen more often when I pray!") Or we can forget how often prayers are answered. If we kept a record of our requests and the answers received, we might be pleasantly surprised. I've kept such a record, and it has provided me with plenty of reasons for prayers of gratitude.

GOD HELPS THOSE
WHO HELP THEMSELVES

This old saying can be recited with cynicism, but there is some truth in it. God may not answer our prayer as we'd like because we should take responsibility for answering that prayer. When we pray, "Lord, help the poor," God may suggest that we help the poor by sharing. When we ask God for good health, God may respond by urging us to give up unhealthy habits and get more exercise. Students who loaf through the semester should not expect God to work the miracle of a passing grade for them in final exams.

You've probably heard the story about the businessman who was going broke. He asked God to let him win the lottery, but he never did. Finally, he shouted at the Almighty, "Why don't you give me a break?" A great gust of wind roared down, a dark cloud hovered overhead, lightning flashed, and a mighty voice thundered, "Give you a break? Why don't you give me a break? At least buy a ticket!"

We must also pray in accord with the ordinary laws of life and common sense. If I pray, "Lord, help our basketball team to win this game," I am asking God to be on our team. God might respond, "Only five players are allowed!" Prayers to win a game ask God to give us an unfair advantage. A better prayer might be, "Lord, help us to do our best." (And this after we've tried to practice, get in good shape, play as a team, and show good sportsmanship.)

PRAYING FOR OTHERS—INTERCESSION

"I've been praying for my son," the mother said, "but God doesn't seem to hear my prayers. My son stopped going to church years ago, and I'm afraid he'll be lost. What more can I do?"

God respects the free will of those for whom we pray. If they have hardened their hearts, they can refuse the grace God offers them in answer to our prayers. Still, persevering prayer can have a great effect on others. Saint Augustine was converted after years of prayer by his mother, Saint Monica. Like a farmer who digs one irrigation ditch after another, sending water to moisten arid fields, a believer praying for a wayward friend establishes conduits through which God's grace can soften the hardest heart.

My Aunt Lena prayed for her son who had stopped practicing his faith. She prayed for forty years, and when I celebrated Mass for her on the occasion of her one hundredth birthday, her son was there, fully reconciled to the Church. Her prayers had smoothed the path back to Jesus for her son, and it was a blessing to see mother and son receive the Body of Christ together.

On a much lighter note, while I was working on this chapter, I received the following e-mail from a friend, Cathy, who lives in Wyoming:

My granddaughter, Bethany, age six, was visiting a few weeks ago. She said she sure wished that her other Gramma would quit smoking. I told her we should pray. So I said a short prayer for her other Gramma and told her that any time she thought of it, she could say, "Jesus, help Gramma quit smoking." And, I told her, we could ask my friends, the monks (at a nearby monastery), to pray, too. I called the monastery the next day. About an hour later, Bethany said, "Oh, can you call the chimps again and ask them to pray that Gramma's friend Christopher will stop smoking too?" "The chimps?!" I was puzzled for just a few seconds...."Oh! You mean the monks?" "Chimps, monks, whatever," she replied. I was about to choke holding in my laughter! So I got out one of the newsletters from the monastery, with pictures, to show her there were people, called monks, not some religious primates! What must she have thought of THIS Gramma, asking chimpanzees to pray for us! Did she think I called the zoo? What a hoot!

Children can bring joy, and laughter, to prayer. If there are children in your life, ask them to pray with you for someone among your family or acquaintances who needs God's help. And whether we pray for others alone or with children, we are following the counsel of Scripture: "First of all, then, I urge that supplications, prayers, intercessions, and thanksgivings be made for everyone, for kings and all who are in high positions, so that we may lead a quiet and peaceable life in all godliness and dignity" (1 Timothy 2:1–2). We are also imitating Jesus, who "is able for all time to save those who approach God through him, since he always lives to make intercession for them" (Hebrews 7:25).

SPIRITUAL GIFTS

I've often heard stories about people who receive distinct messages from God. Others tell of waking in the middle of the night with the certainty that a particular person needs prayer. One woman, thus awakened, knew she had to pray for a friend of her son. She discovered later that, at the very time she was praying, her son's friend was in grave danger, trapped behind enemy lines in Iraq. He escaped, experiencing a strength and guidance that could only be attributed to prayer.

I've never had such spiritual gifts, and perhaps you've never had them either. Does this mean something is wrong with our prayer life? Not at all. Different people have different gifts. Some have a special ability to know what to ask for. Some have a gift of praying for the sick. Some report they can hear God speaking to them. There are many spiritual gifts, and no one possesses them all. Many individuals with many kinds of spiritual gifts make up the body of Christ (1 Corinthians 12:12–31). We are blessed to be members of the body of Christ, and we benefit from the gifts granted to others.

THE POSSIBILITIES ARE INFINITE

Just as scientists are discovering incredible facts about the universe and the complexity of life, so they are uncovering exciting possibilities for prayer. Recent experiments indicate that our brains are designed to contact God. In the sixteenth century, Saint John of the Cross wrote that we can have our most direct experience of God if we detach ourselves from sensory stimuli. Brain scans now show that people deep in contemplation produce a distinct pattern of neural activity where information flowing from the senses slows dramatically and the mind experiences a sensation of unity with God. What Saint John taught has a basis in biology.

Our brains are wired for God in the same way they are wired for light. Seeing light stimulates a part of the brain designed to receive and analyze light. Contemplation stimulates a part of the brain designed to experience union with God.

Gerald Schroeder, a scientist with a doctorate in physics from the Massachusetts Institute of Technology, teaches Scripture in Jerusalem. In his book, *The Science of God*, he moves from a description of creation to the possibilities for joy the Creator holds out to us:

> Let's look at the universe, its cosmic genesis, and see if we can discern hints of a transcendent Creator historically active in the creation. If we do, we can move on and investigate how we might capture the all-too-rare rush of joy sensed when we chance upon the transcendent. Instead of waiting passively for it to happen, imagine being able to have that joy as a permanent partner in life. That would be called getting the most out of life (p. 19).

When we turn to God in prayer of petition, we enter a space where great things can happen. We enter the presence of almighty God. The possibilities are limitless and exciting. There is an old saying that God always answers prayers, but sometimes the answer is "yes," sometimes "no," and sometimes "wait." We place our needs before God and eagerly anticipate an answer, knowing that whatever the response, in God's providence it will be best.

Questions for Discussion and Reflection

What is the most remarkable answer to prayer you've ever received? What has been your greatest disappointment in prayer?

Mike told his friend, Butch, terminally ill with cancer, that he'd be praying for him. Butch replied, "Either way it's win-win for me. If I recover, I get to stay with my family. If I don't recover, I get to go home." What is your opinion about this reply? Have you ever felt this way about the possibility of your own death?

Penny and Scott were trying to sell their house so they could begin construction on the home of their dreams. They prayed for almost three years, and it seemed like God wasn't listening. Then a buyer showed up who wanted to purchase their house for rental purposes. Penny and Scott sold the house in a deal that included their right to rent the house for a year while they built their new home. God's timing was perfect! Have you ever had a similar experience, where waiting for God's time brought unexpected blessings?

ACTIVITIES

Often, as believers become more experienced in the ways of prayer, they find themselves asking for fewer things and are content simply to place their lives in God's hands. Take a few moments and do this now.

Think of someone you know who needs God's help. Place yourself in the company of Jesus and pray for that person.

If there is anything you are worrying about, reflect on this scriptural passage: "Do not worry about anything, but in everything by prayer and supplication with thanksgiving let your requests be made known to God" (Philippians 4:6). Turn your worries over to Jesus and pray about your concerns.

Chapter Five

REMAINING WITH JESUS

❦

F ather Rick Arkfeld, ordained a priest in the diocese of Omaha, Nebraska, in 1962, contracted cancer in the mid-1980s and was told by doctors that he had only a short time left. He made arrangements for his funeral, then proceeded to live another decade. He seemed to gather new energy from his illness and traveled widely to speak, always with much laughter, about life and death and heaven.

As the years rolled on, Father Rick touched many lives with his sense of humor, trust in Jesus, and faith in the face of death. He remarked he'd lived so long after the doctors' grim prognosis that some folks couldn't believe he had cancer. He said with a smile that he wanted his tombstone to read, "I told you I was sick."

Eventually, multiple surgeries so weakened him that he died of congestive heart failure on October 15, 1996. I'm sure he is now assisting through the communion of saints the many people he encouraged during his life on earth.

One of those he encouraged was me. In particular, I was so touched by a talk he gave on prayer that I'd like to share it here. We'll call it...

A CHAIR FOR JESUS

A Catholic priest was checking the patient list for parishioners in a hospital when he noticed the name of a man he'd known in another parish years before. He stopped at his room to say hello and asked how the man, now elderly, was doing. "My doctors say I'm dying," replied the man. "I'm sorry," said the priest. "Oh, don't be," the old man smiled back. "I'm really excited about it. I know I'm going to be with Jesus."

The priest was surprised at the man's answer and asked how he could be so cheerful about death. "Well," he replied, "it goes back a long way. When I was younger I grew very discouraged about prayer. I tried to pray, but Jesus never seemed to be there and I never seemed to get an answer. So I just went through the motions. Then a priest gave a weeklong retreat at our parish and invited us to talk with him. I told him my problem with prayer. 'Oh, that's very common' he said, 'and I can help you, but you'll have to be willing to make a sacrifice.' 'I'll try anything,' I told him, and I meant it.

"The mission priest said, 'You'll have to become like a child. You know how little kids talk to their teddy bears? And get an answer? They use their imagination. Well, Jesus is really there when we pray, but we can't see him, unless we use our imagination. So do this: Choose a room where you have some privacy. Put a chair in the room, and picture Jesus in the chair. See him in his robe and sandals, if you want. Then just talk to him in your own words. Tell him what you're upset about and what you're happy about. Do this every day. Each day it will take less time to get comfortable with Jesus, and easier to talk with him. Then try this: After you have had your say, just be quiet and listen. You'll hear Jesus speak to your heart. God, who made you, can put ideas, memories, and images into your head. That's how God talks to you and answers your prayers.'"

"So I tried it," the old man told the priest-visitor, "and it worked! It wasn't long before Jesus would sit right there and talk with me, and we've become the best of friends. See this chair next to my bed? That's for Jesus. When the doctors told me I would die soon, I waited until they left the room. Then I invited Jesus to come in and sit down, and I told him what the doctors said. 'I know,' he answered, 'I heard them. And I'm happy because we'll soon get to see each other face to face.'"

"That's why I'm excited about dying," the old man continued, "because I can't wait to be with my friend, Jesus." The priest was overwhelmed and, choking back tears, said he wanted to visit again.

But when he returned a few days later, he saw the man's daughter in the hall outside his room, crying. "He just died," she told the priest. "I left his room to get a bite to eat, and when I came back he was gone. I know he was ready, but what bothers me is how he must have suffered in his last moments. When I found him, he was halfway out of bed, and his head was on that chair next to his bed."

The priest took her hand and smiled. "Let's take a minute to talk," he said. "There's a story I need to tell you about that chair."

Public Prayer and Private Prayer

There are many kinds of prayer. The greatest prayer is the one Jesus gave us on the night before he died—the Eucharist. "This is my body," he said, "Do this in memory of me." Any prayer with others has a special value, for Jesus tells us, "[W]here two or three are gathered in my name, I am there among them" (Matthew 18:20).

But Jesus also recommends private prayer, speaking to God heart to heart. "[W]henever you pray, go into your room and shut the door and pray to your Father who is in secret" (Matthew 6:6). Here we will look at many ways of private and public prayer that help us as Catholics to relate to God.

JESUS WANTS TO VISIT WITH US

One day John the Baptist and two of his disciples saw Jesus walk by. John said, "Look, here is the Lamb of God!" Impressed, the disciples followed Jesus. When he noticed them he asked, "What are you looking for?" Taken by surprise, they could only respond, "Where do you live?" Jesus said simply, "Come and see." They accepted the invitation and remained with Jesus that whole day (see John 1:35–39).

In the Book of Revelation (3:20), Jesus addresses a similar invitation to us: "Listen! I am standing at the door, knocking; if you hear my voice and open the door, I will come in to you and eat with you, and you with me."

Jesus knocks at the door of our heart. We ought to welcome him in with enthusiasm. We schedule time to be with friends, so we should set aside time with Jesus. If we feel this is impossible because we are too busy, we should think about the person we most admire and love. If this individual offered to spend fifteen minutes or half an hour with us each day, we would make room in our schedule. Jesus Christ, the Lord of the universe, wishes to visit with us each day. We must find time!

And if you are looking for a way to spend time, to "remain with Jesus," Father Arkfeld's story is a good place to begin. It presents a simple way of conversing with Christ. There are many other ways, which we will now investigate.

ACTS OF PRAYER, WAYS OF PRAYING

How does this chapter on the ways of praying fit with the last two chapters on the four ACTS of prayer? The four kinds of prayer may be compared to four musical compositions or songs. These compositions can be played on different instruments, such as the piano, flute, harp, trumpet, and violin. Acts of adoration, contrition, thanksgiving, and supplication are kinds of prayer that can be offered in many ways, for example, vocal prayer, meditation, centering prayer, contemplation, song, and charismatic prayer. Note, for example, how Father Arkfeld's way of prayer could be used to express the four kinds of prayer—adoration, contrition, thanks, or supplication.

VOCAL PRAYER

The most natural way to pray is to talk to God in our own words, as Father Arkfeld suggests. But I've been surprised on occasion to discover that some Catholics don't know how to do this. I met Michael and Kelley at a parish mission in Colorado. They were in the RCIA program, preparing to be received into the Catholic Church. They had previously been very active in their Protestant denomination and had served as missionaries in Europe. They said, "We have Catholic friends who have never prayed in their own words, and we met many such people when we were in Europe."

Talking to God is really quite simple. We can just speak as we would to any friend. Fancy phrases are not required. We should be open and honest, saying what is on our minds and in our hearts. Whether we are happy or sad, hopeful or depressed, upset or at peace, we can share our feelings with God our Father, Jesus our Savior, and the Holy Spirit our Advocate. We may talk to God silently without moving our lips. We may talk to God in a whisper or in an audible voice. What matters is that we speak from the heart.

While on the subject of talking to God...It's remarkable how many people are shy about using God's name in public prayer, but have no hesitation about using God's name for less sacred purposes. This not only offends God and breaks the second commandment, it causes scandal to others. A teacher in a Catholic school caught little Jeff using God's name carelessly, along with other colorful expressions. "Jeff," she said, "you shouldn't use such words." "Well," Jeff said, "my Dad uses them." "That doesn't matter," replied the teacher. "You don't even know what they mean." "I do too," countered Jeff, "they mean the lawn mower won't start."

If we find ourselves slipping into a careless use of God's name, we might try turning that into prayer. I read a true story about Stephen, a five-year-old, who picked up some bad habits from the kids down the street and began using the Lord's name in vain. Dad promptly gave him a lecture on the second commandment. A few days later, he heard Stephen say, "Oh God!" when he broke his favorite toy truck. Looking up from his newspaper, Dad issued a stern reminder, "Stephen!" Immediately Stephen bowed his head, folded his hands, and said, "Amen."

Vocal prayer may also be expressed in the words of Scripture, in formulas found in prayer books, or in popular prayers. Of the prayers found in Scripture, the Lord's Prayer is most important. Many other scriptural prayers of adoration, contrition, thanks, and supplication may be found in Chapters Three and Four.

There are various kinds of Catholic prayer books, like those given to children on the occasion of their first Communion or those held in the trembling hands of the elderly. Such books offer prayers for every time and circumstance and provide patterns for putting our thoughts and feelings into words.

Popular prayers include the Sign of the Cross, Hail Mary, Glory to the Father, Apostles' Creed, Act of Contrition, Acts of Faith, Hope, and Love, Memorare, Hail Holy Queen, and Grace before and after meals. These prayers have been passed down for centuries and remind us that we are part of a Church whose prayers have gone up to God like incense for two thousand years.

A Catholic prayer that merits special attention is the Way of the Cross. Most Catholic churches display on the walls the Stations of the Cross, traditional scenes from the passion and death of Christ. Catholics may walk from station to station, following in the footsteps of Christ, praying in their own words or from a formula. The Way of the Cross includes vocal and meditative prayer and may be prayed privately or in common. Many parishes schedule times for this devotion during the Lenten season.

Most of us have favorite ways of praying. Among my favorites are the Three-Minute Trinity Prayer, the Hail Mary for peace of soul, and the practice of resting in the presence of Jesus the Healer. The first two are explained here. The third is described in the section, "Imaging Prayer."

THE THREE-MINUTE TRINITY PRAYER

Begin the "Three-Minute Trinity Prayer" by placing yourself in God's presence, adoring Father, Son, and Holy Spirit with the Sign of the Cross and the Glory to the Father. Then turn to Jesus and consider your most serious failing in the past twenty-four hours. Ask Jesus to forgive you. In the second minute, think about the greatest blessing you've received in the past twenty-four hours, and thank God the Father for that blessing. In the third, look ahead to the greatest challenge that faces you in the next twenty-four hours, and ask the Holy Spirit to be your helper and guide as you accept that challenge. I've used this prayer daily for many years. It includes adoration, contrition, thanksgiving, and supplication (ACTS). It can strengthen our relationship with Father, Son, and Holy Spirit, helping us realize that each of us is "the temple of the living God" (2 Corinthians 6:16).

THE HAIL MARY FOR PEACE OF SOUL

Mary is our greatest model of prayer. She was one with Jesus as she carried him in her womb, shared his mortal life until his resurrection, then remained close to him in prayer. Now in his presence forever, she can help us draw strength from Jesus in every difficulty. A prayer I've found very helpful is to replace feelings of anger and frustration with a Hail Mary when I'm upset or tempted to impatience. On some days I say a lot of Hail Marys! But I find that the prayers bring far more peace and happiness than giving in to hostile emotions. I try to remember that Mary, standing at the cross, endured more misunderstanding and hatred in three hours than I will in a lifetime. Mary thereby helps me try to imitate the patience of Jesus in difficult times and to find peace of soul. (And I must remember that others are probably repeating Hail Marys because I am testing their patience!)

In our busy world, it is easy to magnify minor irritations and let family members or friends get on our nerves. This damages relationships and gives us high blood pressure as well as other health problems. Turning aggravations into prayer minimizes the damage and asks Mary to help us become more like her Son.

MEDITATION

The *Catechism of the Catholic Church* explains meditation as systematic reflection on the truths of faith found in Scripture, the liturgy, spiritual writings, creation, and events of history. We incorporate these truths into our lives by applying them to our own situation. We use thought, imagination, emotion, desire, and memory to unite ourselves more closely to the heart, mind, and will of Jesus (2705–2708).

In previous chapters we have shown that God speaks to us in many ways. If we are to recognize God's voice and presence, we must learn how to be attentive. This is not easy in our modern world. The rush, the noise, the constant distractions keep us at a frantic pace where we find it difficult to heed the message of Scripture: "Be still before the LORD, and wait patiently for him" (Psalm 37:7).

We need a time and place for meditation. Some people rise

early to pray for an hour, half-hour, or fifteen minutes. Others pray during lunch hour or just before retiring. The important thing is to schedule a time and be faithful to it. The ideal place for meditation is before the Blessed Sacrament, but this might be impossible or difficult for many. A quiet room or corner of one's house may be the next best option. We might decorate that place with a crucifix, statues, or religious paintings. Such surroundings can help us keep our mind and hearts focused on God during prayer.

Next, we need a way of quieting ourselves and becoming aware of God's presence. You may wish to use the following five-step method:

1. Sit quietly in a firm chair. Keep your back straight. Close your eyes and become aware of any tension. Progressively relax the muscles in your face, neck, shoulders, arms, torso, legs, and feet. Reflect on the words of Jesus, "Peace I leave with you; my peace I give to you" (John 14:27).

2. Pay attention to your breathing. If it is shallow, deepen it. If it is rapid, slow it down. Breathe deeply and think about the first breath you took as an infant and about the last breath you will take on this earth. Reflect on this verse of Scripture: "The spirit of God has made me, / and the breath of the Almighty gives me life" (Job 33:4).

3. Be attentive to the sounds of life around you—a bird singing, a breeze stirring the trees, voices in the distance, a car passing. Consider how all activity and life have their origin in God. Meditate on these words: "For he is our God... / O that today you would listen to his voice!" (Psalm 95:7).

4. Be sensitive to the experience of touch. Feel the softness of your clothing, the press of the chair against your body and of the floor against your feet, the gentle embrace of the air surrounding you. Think about these words of Saint Paul, "In him we live and move and have our being" (Acts 17:28).

5. Feel your heart beating. Recall how it sends life-giving oxygen to every cell in your body. Think too of how the heart is a symbol of love, just as necessary for life as air itself. Ponder these words of Scripture: "[T]he LORD set his heart on you" (Deuteronomy 7:7); "you shall love the Lord your God with all your heart" (Mark 12:30).

KINDS OF MEDITATION

There are many different kinds of meditation. Perhaps the best known is that of Saint Ignatius of Loyola. After directing our attention to God, we reflect, for example, on some scene from the gospels. We place ourselves in the scene, imagining the sights, sounds, scents, tastes, and touches. We talk with Jesus. We make a resolution to imitate Jesus more closely in some practical way as a result of our reflection.

Here, for example, is how we might meditate on the birth of Jesus as described in the Gospel of Luke, 2:1–21, using Saint Ignatius' method.

You imagine yourself in a caravan traveling from Galilee toward Jerusalem. You walk just behind Joseph, who is leading a small donkey that carries his pregnant wife. You hear Joseph ask Mary, "Are you comfortable?" She smiles weakly and nods. They, like many in the caravan, are moving southward to register for yet another census. "This isn't what we had planned, Mary," says Joseph, "but we must obey the emperor's decree. God is guiding us. Just a few weeks ago two old men at the well were discussing the birthplace of the Messiah. One of them argued that the prophet Micah pointed to Bethlehem. I thought he was mistaken. Now here we are, on our way to Bethlehem."

In Bethlehem they find no room at the inn, and

continue on. In prayer you remain with them. As Mary's time draws near, Joseph resolves to find a place with shelter and privacy. He discovers a hillside cave where sheep huddle in bad weather. In this cave the Son of God is born. Mary holds her child a long while, then hands him to Joseph. "He's beautiful," Mary says. "Yes," smiles Joseph. "He looks just like his mother!"

A sudden noise outside the cave startles them. A band of shepherds enters, and you join them. "I'm sorry to frighten you. May we come in?" asks the leader of the group. "We're only poor shepherds, but God sent angels to tell us of the birth of this child." "Come," says Joseph, "We are poor too, and God loves the poor. I am Joseph, a carpenter. This is Mary. Our child's name is Jesus."

You stand in awe with the shepherds, gazing at the infant. The cave is small and there are unpleasant odors, but Joseph has spread clean straw on the ground under the manger where the baby lies. He smiles, invites you to step closer, and asks if you'd like to hold the child. You take Jesus and hold him close, knowing that your arms embrace God.

Now you move back to the present. Joseph joins you at your place of prayer. He smiles and says, "What a great blessing it was to hold the baby Jesus in my arms, to kiss him, to feel the scent of his breath! But remember that at holy Communion you hold Jesus in your hands, receive him into your heart, and are joined to him in a way I never enjoyed...until heaven, that is."

In such a meditation, we enter as deeply as possible into the events of Scripture. We use all our faculties, our mind, imagination, memory, feelings, and will. We then try to apply the lessons of Scripture to our own lives. For example, we might consider how Jesus entered the world in Bethlehem, and try to realize that Jesus dwells in people today. What we do to them, we do to Jesus (Matthew 25:40). Do we recognize the presence of Jesus in the members of our family? In others? Do we try to treat everyone the way we would treat Jesus himself?

We might also reflect on the real presence of Jesus in holy Communion. In the imaginary conversation with Saint Joseph, we are invited to treasure each Communion as an opportunity to hold Jesus as close as he was held at Bethlehem by Mary and Joseph.

We end our meditation by making a practical resolution based on some of the above considerations. It might be one of the following: Today I will avoid any harshness toward members of my family. Today I will help clean the table after dinner and do the dishes. Sunday when I receive holy Communion, I will imagine myself in the stable-cave at Bethlehem holding Jesus in my arms, and I will adore and thank him as Mary and Joseph surely did.

REFLECTIVE READING

Reflective reading is a method of meditation where we read from the Bible, the *Catechism of the Catholic Church*, the writings of the Holy Father, or a spiritual book, pausing to think and pray each time some passage inspires us. This differs from the method of Saint Ignatius where we focus on one incident in the life of Jesus and use all our faculties to spotlight it from every angle. In reflective reading, we tend to cover more territory in less depth than when we follow Ignatius. However, our emphasis in reflective reading should be more on prayer than on reading. We often pause to ponder a point that touches our heart, we consider how it might fit into the Father's providential plan for our lives, we talk to Jesus about this, and we ask the Holy Spirit to guide us in applying it to everyday living.

IMAGING PRAYER

Imaging prayer is a form of mental prayer that is built on images rather than words. We praise God by picturing ourselves kneeling before the throne of God in heaven. We thank God by visualizing the blessings we have received as gifts flowing from God. We express sorrow for sin by mentally standing at the cross of Jesus. We make petitions by forming images of our needs and putting them before God. We pray for others by picturing Jesus standing next to them, placing his hands on them and blessing them.

Imaging prayer is a beautiful way to end the day. Before you fall asleep, form a mental image of Jesus the Healer coming to your bedside. Picture him placing his hands on your head to comfort and heal you. Picture him delivering you from any physical illness or pain, any harmful feelings such as fear, depression, resentment, anxiety, and hatred. Image Jesus as he shares his love with you while you sleep, as he fills your whole being with the fruit of the Holy Spirit mentioned by Saint Paul in Galatians 5:22–23: love, joy, peace, patience, kindness, generosity, faithfulness, gentleness, and self-control.

You may use imaging as a prayer for others. Picture Jesus standing at their bedsides, giving them his healing and peace. It is worth noting that physicians can do great works of healing through surgery when we are asleep from anesthesia. Jesus, who never sleeps, can do wonderful works of healing—for body, mind, emotions, and soul, as we sleep. Imaging prayer is a powerful way to open yourself to his healing presence. I've been using this prayer of Jesus the Healer every night for decades, and I've found it to be a source of great blessings. It's also a much better way to get a good night's rest than counting sheep!

CONTEMPLATION

Contemplation, according to the *Catechism of the Catholic Church* (2697–2724), is dwelling in God's presence, focusing our attention on the Lord. The psalmist advises, "Be still, and know that I am God!" (Psalm 46:10). We give God our time and ourselves, and seek union with Father, Son, and Holy Spirit through their grace and love. We put our faith in God, unite our will to God's, and become one with the prayer of Jesus. Here less attention is paid to what we do in prayer, more to what God does in us. Studying this entire section of the *Catechism* will help anyone achieve a better understanding of contemplation as it is practiced in the Catholic Church.

In describing contemplation, the *Catechism* makes a reference to Saint Jean-Baptiste-Marie Vianney, the curé of Ars in nineteenth-century France.

> Contemplation is a *gaze* of faith, fixed on Jesus. "I look at him and he looks at me": this is what a certain peasant of Ars in the time of his holy curé used to say while praying before the tabernacle. This focus on Jesus is a renunciation of self. His gaze purifies our heart; the light of the countenance of Jesus illumines the eyes of our heart and teaches us to see everything in the light of his truth and his compassion for all men. Contemplation also turns its gaze on the mysteries of the life of Christ. Thus it learns the "interior knowledge of our Lord," the more to love him and follow him (2715).

In contemplation we strive to become more attentive to the work of the Holy Spirit in us as we pray. "Likewise the Spirit helps us in our weakness; for we do not know how to pray as we ought, but that very Spirit intercedes with sighs too deep for words. And God, who searches the heart, knows what is the mind of the Spirit, because the Spirit intercedes for the saints according to the will of God" (Romans 8:26–27). Contemplation means resting in the Spirit, becoming aware of the presence of the Holy Spirit as the guest of our souls. Jesus promised on the night before he died that "the Advocate, the Holy Spirit, whom the Father will send in my name, will teach you everything, and remind you of all that I have said to you" (John 14:26).

We learn here from Jesus that contemplation is Trinitarian prayer. Saint Paul emphasizes this in a marvelous passage that shows how contemplation looks to God the Father for the gift of grace. The Holy Spirit strengthens and enlightens our "inner being." Then we are able to recognize Christ dwelling in our hearts and we grow in his love. Again, the emphasis in contemplation is more on what God does in us than on our own activity.

For this reason I bow my knees before the Father, from whom every family in heaven and on earth takes its name. I pray that, according to the riches of his glory, he may grant that you may be strengthened in your inner being with power through his Spirit, and that Christ may dwell in your hearts through faith, as you are being rooted and grounded in love. I pray that you may have the power to comprehend, with all the saints, what is the breadth and length and height and depth, and to know the love of Christ that surpasses knowledge, so that you may be filled with all the fullness of God (Ephesians 3:14–19).

Contemplation, as the *Catechism* points out, is not easy. "The choice of the *time and duration of the prayer* arises from a determined will, revealing the secrets of the heart. One does not undertake contemplative prayer only when one has the time: one makes time for the Lord, with the firm determination not to give up, no matter what trials and dryness one may encounter"

(2710). Archbishop Fulton Sheen used to tell how he spent an hour in the presence of the Blessed Sacrament every day. Once, after a long airline flight and a difficult day, he found a Catholic church and went in to make his holy hour. He promptly fell asleep, and woke up more than an hour later. It was now time for an appointment and he had to leave. "I asked the Lord," he said, "if this counted as my holy hour." According to Archbishop Sheen, the Lord replied, "Well, that's how Peter, James, and John spent their hour with me in the Garden of Gethsemane!"

CENTERING PRAYER

Centering prayer is a form of contemplative prayer that has become popular in recent times. It is built on the reality that prayer can go beyond expressing thoughts and feelings verbally. Centering prayer opens mind, heart, and awareness to God, who is always near, and looks to God to bestow the gift of divine presence and love.

Centering prayer focuses on the recitation of a "sacred word" that expresses our desire to be open to God. The word might be something like "Abba," "Father," "Jesus," or "Holy Spirit." We begin by sitting comfortably, back straight, eyes closed, and making the intention of opening ourselves to God's presence. We recite the sacred word peacefully, letting go of all thoughts or feelings. If thoughts or feelings begin to intrude, we gently return to the sacred word. Typically, a minimum of twenty minutes is recommended for this kind of prayer. In the last two minutes, we remain silent as a way of allowing the time of contemplation to flow into our daily life.

Catholic teachers of centering prayer emphasize that it is not a form of relaxation or New-Age meditation. It is rather a way to communicate with God. It emulates the prophet, Elijah, who found God, not in wind or fire or earthquake, but in the "sound of sheer silence" (1 Kings 19:12).

It is important to make a distinction between Christian centering prayer and the centering techniques of Eastern religions. Eastern religions do not accept Jesus Christ as the Savior of the world. Eastern forms of centering prayer, like transcendental meditation, tend to seek God as an impersonal state of being, one with all reality. Catholic Christians know God as Father, Son, and Holy Spirit. We believe in God as Creator, Savior, and Advocate, distinct from and infinitely superior to anything in creation.

Our efforts to become aware of the presence of the Trinity within us are based on the words of Jesus. At the Last Supper, Jesus promised that the Holy Spirit would live in us: "And I will ask the Father, and he will give you another Advocate, to be with you forever. This is the Spirit of truth....You know him, because he abides with you, and he will be in you" (John 14:16–17). He then assured us that he and the Father live in us as well: "Those who love me will keep my word, and my Father will love them, and we will come to them and make our home with them" (John 14:23).

Here is how Sheila, a young wife and mother, describes her experience of centering prayer:

> Prayer itself has always been a big part of my life, but it's always been me doing all of the talking. It wasn't until centering prayer that I have learned to "be still" and let God talk to me. First, I give "my intention" to be present with God and then give my "consent" for him to be present with me. After that I may use my "sacred word" to keep my attention with God, and then I just trust in God to be with me.
>
> I have experienced God speaking to me and giving me answers I've needed, but only when I've quieted my mind and opened my heart to him. Sometimes, however, I can just sit with God in complete silence and he fills me with such joy and deep love. The relationship I've developed

with God through centering prayer has certainly become one of deeper love and of constant longing for him.

THE JESUS PRAYER

The Jesus Prayer has a long history in Eastern Christianity dating back to at least the fifth century. It consists in reciting, "Lord, Jesus Christ, Son of God, have mercy on me, a sinner," or in repeating the name of Jesus. In the Eastern tradition, monks might recite the prayer hundreds of times a day, or even constantly, in an effort to follow the counsel of Saint Paul: "[P]ray without ceasing" (1 Thessalonians 5:17). The Jesus Prayer, while originating in the East, has become widely known in the Roman Catholic Church over the past one hundred years and is used by many Catholics today.

This prayer is scriptural because it calls on the name of Jesus, who saved us by his death on the cross. "Therefore God also highly exalted him / and gave him the name / that is above every name, / so that at the name of Jesus / every knee should bend, / in heaven and on earth and under the earth, / and every tongue should confess / that Jesus Christ is Lord, / to the glory of God the Father" (Philippians 2:9–11) The prayer itself is based on several scriptural passages: the humble prayer of the tax collector in the temple, "God, be merciful to me, a sinner!" (Luke 18:13), and the plea of the blind man near Jericho, "Jesus, Son of David, have mercy on me!" (Luke 18:38).

Continued repetition of the Jesus Prayer is meant to bring us into an intimate union with God at every moment. The prayer becomes an expression of our heart's desire for God. That is why the Jesus Prayer is sometimes called "the prayer of the heart." Ideally, it will help bring us to the point where we live as God's children, for "God has sent the Spirit of his Son into our hearts, crying, 'Abba! Father!'" (Galatians 4:6).

PRAYER JOURNALS

Some people keep prayer journals, a daily record of prayer, and may make their prayer to God in writing. If we can send thoughts and feelings to people through letters, we can direct them to God in prayer journals. There are many ways to keep and use prayer journals. Perhaps the most common way is simply to write your thoughts and prayers of adoration, contrition, thanksgiving, and supplication as they occur. You may wish to return to past journals as a source of prayer and as a way of discovering how often God does answer prayer.

PRAYER IN COMMON

Most methods of prayer may be used not only by individuals but also by groups of people and so become forms of common (communal) prayer (CCC 2790–2793). There is a special value to prayer with others, as we learn from Jesus, "Again, truly I tell you, if two of you agree on earth about anything you ask, it will be done for you by my Father in heaven. For where two or three are gathered in my name, I am there among them" (Matthew 18:19–20). As the *Catechism* points out, Jesus also "teaches us to make prayer in common for all our brethren. For he did not say 'my Father' who art in heaven, but 'our' Father, offering petitions for the common Body" (2768). The first Christians recognized the importance of prayer in common for "[t]hey devoted themselves to the apostles' teaching and fellowship, to the breaking of bread and the prayers" (Acts 2:42).

When people pray together they demonstrate their love for one another. They are living signs of the two great commandments: love of God and love of neighbor. Also, people pray for one another when they pray together, and the power of their prayer is multiplied. Jesus came to bring people together in love

(John 17), and this is expressed beautifully through prayer in common.

The Church's official communal prayer is the liturgy. (*Liturgy* comes from a Greek word meaning "a work on behalf of people"). It includes the Mass, sacraments, benediction, *Book of Blessings*, and Liturgy of the Hours. Sunday Mass is the heart of all prayer, and many Catholics attend daily Mass as well. All celebrations of the sacraments allow us to pray for ourselves and others at key moments in life. Benediction is adoration, through song and prayer, of Christ present in the Blessed Sacrament. The *Book of Blessings* is a collection of prayers asking God to bless people and things. The Liturgy of the Hours is the Church's daily prayer said by priests, religious, and many laypeople. We will study liturgical prayer in detail in Chapter Six.

Many Catholic parishes have prayer groups that meet regularly. Some recite the rosary. Others study the Bible, then pray and sing together. Still others participate together in various kinds of contemplative prayer, such as centering prayer.

There are Catholic charismatic prayer groups that emphasize devotion to the Holy Spirit, the Bible, and communal prayer services. They focus on the gifts of the Holy Spirit, including praying in tongues, healing, and prophecy (1 Corinthians 12–14). Speaking in tongues can be a sign of the presence of the Holy Spirit, as can other more "ordinary" gifts like teaching, healing, discernment, assistance, and administration (1 Corinthians 12:27–31). But it must be remembered that the two surest signs of the Spirit's presence and activity are faith and love. In 1 Corinthians 12:3 Saint Paul states: "[N]o one can say 'Jesus is Lord' except by the Holy Spirit." In 1 Corinthians 12:27—13:13, he describes love as the greatest gift of the Spirit. Therefore, those who can say with faith that Jesus is Lord, and those who truly love others have received the Holy Spirit.

Many retreat and renewal movements encourage Catholics to pray together. Some religious orders sponsor retreats for laypeople. There are Marriage Encounter Weekends for married couples, Teens Encounter Christ retreats for young people, and Beginning Again Weekends for the widowed and divorced. Such movements encourage participants to meet for prayer and reflection on a regular basis.

Singing is an important form of common prayer. It is often a part of liturgical prayer, especially the Mass. Through singing, we direct melody and words to God as adoration, contrition, thanksgiving, and supplication. Musical accompaniment and music as background for reflection have been important elements of worship since biblical times, as Psalm 150 indicates. (We may use music in private prayer also. Some listen to recorded religious music as a way to lift mind and heart to God, and some sing favorite hymns to express their feelings to God.)

FAMILY PRAYER

In today's world there is a special need for family prayer (CCC 2685). "The family that prays together stays together." Modern families must realize that prayer is not a luxury, but a necessity. If they are not praying together, they must examine their priorities, rearrange their schedules, and pray together. We find time for things that are important, and we simply must find time for prayer. Even the busiest families should find a few minutes to read and discuss the Bible, say a decade of the rosary, or pray about the day's events.

I tell couples and families: If you are not praying together, make a resolution to do so. But begin with a resolution you can keep. Resolve to pray the Our Father together every day. If you cannot find twenty seconds a day to say this prayer together, your lives are seriously out of kilter. So make this decision: We will pray the Lord's Prayer together every day. After you do this for a while, ask Jesus to guide you to the kind of family prayer he wants for you. Great blessings are in store for families that pray together.

PRAY ALWAYS

Jesus tells us that we need to "pray always" (Luke 18:1). The *Catechism of the Catholic Church* offers an explanation of Jesus' meaning when it states that "the life of prayer is the habit of being in the presence of...God and in communion with him" (2565). As we grow closer to Jesus, we learn to live in God's presence. We schedule special times for prayer, but we also develop habits of speaking to God as we would to any friend. Each day offers many opportunities for such prayer: waiting at stop lights or in traffic, standing in checkout lines, sitting in physicians' offices, driving to and from work (turn off the radio, talk to Jesus, or play Bible tapes or religious music).

Then there are prayer reminders such as cemeteries, where we say a prayer for the deceased, or Catholic churches, where we whisper a word of adoration to Jesus in the Blessed Sacrament. When we hear the sirens of emergency vehicles, we might pray for victims as well as for those involved in often dangerous work of helping others in trouble. Another reminder might be finding a penny, with its prayer, "In God We Trust." The possibilities for prayer are endless, and it can be fun to discover new opportunities to talk to God and pray always.

"PRAY AS YOU CAN"

Some of the best advice on prayer I've heard was given by Sister Delores in a discussion about ways of praying. It was, "Pray as you can, not as you can't." Our Catholic prayer tradition offers wonderful resources for prayer, suggests many ways to pray, and offers us the wisdom of two thousand years of experienced teachers. In this chapter, we've looked at many patterns for vocal and mental prayer. At one time or another, I've used all these patterns. At one time or another, one kind of mental prayer seems more effective than others. Use those that work for you, that help you draw near to Father, Son, and Holy Spirit.

I see our Catholic prayer tradition as something like a restaurant buffet where all kinds of delicious and healthful foods are available. Try them all! Ask Jesus to guide you in prayer, to bring you to the Father, to send the Holy Spirit, who will help you to pray as you ought. Eventually, prayer will lead you to the point where you see God in everything good, where you live in the presence of God, in whom "we live and move and have our being" (Acts 17:28). Prayer will make you one with Jesus, and you can say with Saint Paul, "it is no longer I who live, but it is Christ who lives in me" (Galatians 2:20).

QUESTIONS FOR
DISCUSSION AND REFLECTION

Of all the ways of prayer mentioned in this chapter, what are your favorites? Are there ways of prayer you've used that are not referred to in this chapter? If so, what are they?

Jackie had a habit of talking to herself. One day, she reflected on Paul's words, "Pray without ceasing," and she decided to bring God into the conversation. It has been a great blessing to her. She now talks to God about everything, and God has blessed her with many insights and answers to prayer. Do you ever talk to yourself? Could you bring God into the conversation? Do you think this is a good way to "pray without ceasing?" Can you think of other ways?

Elaine said that she would like to make a one-day retreat at home and was looking for suggestions about how she might do this. What suggestions would you make to her after reading this chapter? What are some other elements of such a retreat that might foster and support forms of prayer?

After hearing a talk on prayer, Margie said, "Since the talk, my husband and I have been praying together every night. We used to pray together when we first got married and then did it with the kids when they were little, but stopped once they were older." In various ways, God encourages couples or families to pray together. What has encouraged you to pray with your family? What difficulties have you encountered? How might you overcome these difficulties? What do you think of the suggestions for family prayer in this chapter?

ACTIVITIES

Find a quiet place and use the five-step method for coming to an awareness of God's presence as described in the section, "Meditation."

Tom explains how he began to meditate on the gospels, using the method of Saint Ignatius. "Before this I never imagined myself at the crucifixion. But now I can, I see the tearful mourners, Mary, and the Apostles. To touch the cross, to see Jesus and look into his eyes, to thank him, personally. To express my sorrow for my sins and my love for him. This is a very powerful, personal way for me to be in touch with God during my prayers."

Try this meditation. Find a quiet place. Take a few moments to relax and focus on God's presence. Then picture yourself at the crucifixion of Jesus. See him hanging on the cross. Look at the crowd standing around, some weeping, some mocking, some indifferent. Listen to Jesus as he speaks from the cross. Hear the sobbing of Jesus' friends, the mockery from his enemies. Touch the wood of Christ's cross. Feel the temperature drop as clouds roll in and the wind begins to blow. Notice the smell of rain, and taste the raindrops on your tongue. Look into Christ's eyes, and thank him for his great love. Express sorrow for your sins and the sins of the world. Tell Christ of your love for him and your desire to bring his love to the world. Then speak to him about anything else that seems important.

Chapter Six

LITURGICAL PRAYER

❧

Jesus had a great sense of humor. Many of his sayings must come with a smile. "Again I tell you, it is easier for a camel to go through the eye of a needle than for someone who is rich to enter the kingdom of God" (Matthew 19:24). We laugh as we think of a camel struggling to slip through a needle's eye, and yet the gentle humor of Jesus teaches an important truth. Wealth can distract us from our eternal destiny.

And another saying, "Why do you see the speck in your neighbor's eye, but do not notice the log in your own eye?" (Luke 6:41). We can't help but smile at the ridiculous image of someone with a huge log in his eye, wanting to remove a tiny speck from the eye of another. But then we realize..."Jesus is talking about me, and how I notice the faults of others far more easily than my own."

Sometimes Jesus' humor is subtle, as in an incident that occurred soon after his resurrection (Luke 24:13–35). Two disciples were on their way to the town of Emmaus, about seven miles from Jerusalem. They were sadly discussing the events that had taken place the past few days when Jesus joined them. Showing his sense of humor, he concealed his identity from them and asked what they were talking about. They stopped in their tracks. "What?" questioned one of them, Cleopas by name, "Are you the only stranger in Jerusalem who doesn't know the things that have been going on?" Jesus (the very one to whom all these things had happened!) pretended to have no idea. "What things?" he asked.

They proceeded to tell him about how Jesus had been arrested, condemned, and crucified. They added that some women had gone to the tomb that morning, found it empty, and reported a vision of angels who told them Jesus was alive.

The sadness that gripped these two disciples was evidence that they placed little confidence in the story. Further evidence may be found in Jesus' response: "How foolish you are, and how slow to believe the prophets!" He went on to explain all the Scripture passages that foretold his passion, death, and resurrection. Then, as they neared Emmaus, Jesus once again showed his sense of humor, pretending to leave his two companions. But by now they were entranced with the words of this stranger and begged him not to go. "It's getting late," they said. "Come and stay with us. We'll buy dinner for you!" So Jesus joined them at table. There he "took bread, blessed and broke it, and gave it to them."

At the breaking of the bread, the two disciples recognized Jesus. He then vanished. Amazed and joyful, they recalled how their hearts had burned within them as Jesus explained the Scriptures. They rushed seven miles in the darkness back to Jerusalem. They told the apostles how Jesus had opened the Scriptures to them and how they had recognized him in the breaking of the bread.

This encounter on the road to Emmaus, the first Mass celebrated after the resurrection (CCC 1347), tells us a great deal about liturgical prayer. The risen Lord proclaimed the Scriptures, then made his presence known in the breaking of the bread. This event demonstrates the unique power of liturgical prayer. Here Jesus speaks to us through the Scriptures and touches us with his presence. The *Catechism of the Catholic Church* (1070) explains it in this way:

> The liturgy then is rightly seen as an exercise of the priestly office of Jesus Christ....In it full public worship is performed by the Mystical Body of Jesus Christ, that

is, by the Head and his members. From this it follows
that every liturgical celebration, because it is an action
of Christ the priest and of his Body which is the Church,
is a sacred action surpassing all others. No other action
of the Church can equal its efficacy by the same title and
to the same degree.

PRAYER TO THE HIGHEST POWER

Because the liturgy is an action of Jesus Christ, it is prayer to the
highest power. Liturgy always includes Scripture, and so Jesus
speaks to us through the inspired words of the Bible. When we
respond in prayer, we respond as the body of Christ, joined to
Jesus our head. Because we pray as members of Christ's body,
our prayer is raised to a new level. Here more than anywhere else,
God speaks and we respond!

Of all liturgical prayers, the Mass comes first. The *Catechism*
states that the Eucharist is the source and summit of our Christian
life because it contains Jesus Christ himself (1324). The Mass is
meal and sacrifice as well as prayer. Here we will briefly discuss
the Mass as prayer. For a complete explanation of the Mass, see
We Worship: A Guide to the Catholic Mass (bibliography).

THE MASS AS PRAYER

God speaks to us through the Scriptures because God inspired
them. We may respond to God using the words of Scripture or
other prayers. But at Mass, there is a unique presence of Jesus
both in the speaking of God's Word and in our response. The
Catechism states that Jesus

> ...is present in his word since it is he himself who speaks
> when the holy Scriptures are read in the Church. [And]
> he is present when the Church prays and sings, for he has

promised "where two or three are gathered together in my name there am I in the midst of them" (1088; Matthew 18:20).

LISTENING ATTENTIVELY TO JESUS

Before we consider our response to God in words of adoration, contrition, thanksgiving, and supplication, we should consider how God speaks to us. At Mass, Scripture is proclaimed from the *Lectionary* and a book of the gospels. Sunday readings include a first reading (usually selected from the Old Testament), a responsorial psalm, a second reading from New Testament books, a gospel verse, and a gospel reading. Weekday readings always include a gospel passage, usually preceded by one reading from other Scripture books, a responsorial psalm, and a gospel verse.

We need to appreciate better the treasure that is ours in the Scripture readings. We must be attentive. This is not easy and requires consistent effort. We moderns are accustomed to noise and fast-moving action. We may find it difficult to concentrate during the readings.

You may have heard the story about the three brothers who had done well in business. As their mother's eightieth birthday approached, they met to discuss the gifts they planned for her. The first brother said, "I bought Momma a Mercedes limousine and a driver to take her wherever she wants to go." The second said, "I bought Momma a forty-room mansion." The third said, "You know how Momma loves the Bible, but her eyes are failing. Well, I bought Momma a parrot that can recite the whole Bible. It took six monks five years to train the bird, and I had to donate a million a year to the monastery to make it possible. But Momma's worth every penny. All she has to do is call out the chapter and verse, and the parrot will recite it." A week after the party, the boys received their thank-you notes. The first read, "Dear Marvin, thank you for the car. Of course, you know I don't like to travel and the driver is so rude I can't stand to be with him. But thanks anyway. Love, Momma." The second boy read, "Dear Melvin, thank you for the house. Of course, I can only live in one of the forty rooms, but I have to clean the other thirty-nine. But thanks anyway. Love, Momma." The third boy read, "Dear Milburn, you were the only one of my boys who knew what your old Momma really wanted. The chicken was delicious!"

A lot of Scripture went up in a cloud of feathers! And at every Mass, a lot of Scripture can go up in a cloud of distractions and inattention. How can we be more attentive? I like to suggest that we should listen to the readings the way we'd listen to instructions about how to pack our own parachute. Also, it can be helpful to listen with the intention of remembering at least one passage from each reading that we can apply to our own life. Above all, we should focus on the reality that Jesus is the one who addresses us, no matter who the reader might be. We might even try picturing Jesus standing there at the lectern, dressed in robe and sandals, reading to us as he did to the congregation at the synagogue in Nazareth (Luke 4:16–30). Hopefully, we will give him a better welcome than did his townspeople!

OUR RESPONSE TO GOD'S PRESENCE AND WORD

When we respond to God at Mass, we use all four ACTS of prayer. We adore, express contrition, give thanks, and offer our supplications. We respond by praying out loud with the congregation, by praying quietly when the priest says prayers that are reserved to the celebrant, by silence at appropriate times, and by singing.

Singing requires special attention, as hymns may express each of the four kinds of prayer, sometimes all four within a single verse. Mass often begins with a song, and other hymns and sacred music may form part of our Eucharistic celebration. Different parts of the Mass may be sung, and we should remember that singing is praying twice—through the words and the music. We must, therefore, view our singing not as a performance, but as prayer. We should make a conscious effort to heed the meaning of the words and to address them to God.

We can easily recognize certain parts of the Mass as prayer by their titles, for example, the collect (opening prayer), prayer over the offerings, and prayer after communion. The penitential rite is a prayer of contrition. The *Gloria* (Glory to God in the highest) is a prayer of adoration, and also includes expressions of contrition, thanks, and supplication. The responsorial psalm is a meditation on the first reading from Scripture, and it might include any or all of the four ACTS of prayer. The Creed is an expression of our belief and is both a prayer of adoration and a petition for stronger faith. The prayer of the faithful places before God our needs and those of the world. The preparation of the gifts begins the Liturgy of the Eucharist. We are reminded that *eucharist* means "thanksgiving" as the priest says, "Let us give thanks to the Lord our God." The various eucharistic prayers are praise, contrition, thanksgiving, and petition, as is the Lord's Prayer. The "Deliver us" and prayer for peace allow us to place our supplications for personal and world peace before God. Communion is a time of union with Jesus, a time to speak to him about anything and to consider how he joins us to himself and to the Church. The Eucharist fittingly closes with "Thanks be to God," and perhaps a final hymn.

As we pray the Mass, it is helpful to be attentive to the ACTS of prayer. For example, we might be surprised at the frequency of acts of contrition. The penitential rite is obviously an acknowledgment of sin and a prayer for pardon. But the *Gloria* immediately offers an opportunity to honor Jesus as our savior, as the lamb who takes away the sins of the world. So we make our plea, "have mercy on us." The Liturgy of the Word makes frequent references to the reality of sin. The silent prayer of the priest before reading the gospel asks for salvation from sin: "Cleanse my heart and my lips, almighty God, that I may worthily proclaim your holy Gospel." After reading the gospel, the priest kisses the book and prays, "Through the words of the Gospel may our sins be wiped away." The prayer of the faithful may include petitions for forgiveness. As the priest prepares the gifts, he bows at the altar and quietly prays that our sacrifice be pleasing to the Lord God. Then there is the washing of hands, expressing a desire for interior purification: "Wash me, O Lord, from my iniquity and cleanse me from my sin." At the consecration, we are reminded that Jesus shed his blood "for the forgiveness of sins." At the Lord's Prayer, we ask God to "forgive us our trespasses, as we forgive those who trespass against us." Then we pray that God will keep us "free from sin." We pray or sing, "Lamb of God, you take away the sins of the world, have mercy on us." Then the priest quietly says a prayer including the words, "free me from all my sins and from every evil," or asking that communion bring "protection in mind and body," not condemnation. He holds the host and chalice before the people and says, "Behold the Lamb of God, behold him who takes away the sins of the world." We respond, "Lord, I am not worthy that you should enter under my roof, but only say the word and my soul shall be healed."

If we pay close attention to all the parts and prayers of the Mass, we find frequent acts of adoration, thanksgiving, and supplication. Being aware of the ACTS of prayer as we attend the Eucharist can help us pray the Mass with more meaning and devotion.

RESPONSE AND POSTURE AS PRAYER

A kind of prayer used often at Mass, but sometimes not perceived as prayer, is the pattern of responses said by the congregation. The priest says, "The Lord be with you," or a similar phrase. The congregation responds, "And with your spirit." These words are more than friendly greetings. They are prayers asking God to be close to those we address. "Thanks be to God" and "Praise to you, Lord Jesus Christ" are prayers of grateful adoration to God who has spoken to us in the Scriptures. "Blessed be God forever" is praise and thanks. "Amen," as we have seen, is a Hebrew word, a prayer meaning "so be it," or, more personally, "I proclaim my belief in this truth." "Alleluia" is repeated before the gospel, allowing us to "praise the Lord" for the beauty of Jesus' life and teaching.

The postures we take at Eucharist should be prayer. When we stand, we are not just "standing around" as we might in a lobby. We are taking an ancient posture of prayer, addressing God as the source of all good. When we sit, we are not just taking a comfortable position as we might at a theater. Rather, we are placing ourselves in an attentive attitude to hear God's word. When we kneel, we imitate Jesus in his humble petition to the Father in the Garden of Gethsemane (Luke 22:41). When we genuflect or bow, we adore the Lord who is truly present among us. These postures and gestures are sacramental prayers, physical signs of inward dispositions of worship.

In word, song, silence, posture, and gesture, we pray the Mass. But we must always strive to be attentive. We should frequently ask for the aid of the Holy Spirit, who "helps us in our weakness; for we do not know how to pray as we ought" (Romans 8:26).

THE OTHER SACRAMENTS AS PRAYER

We've all been to baptisms and confirmations, celebrated the weddings of friends, and attended funeral Masses of departed relatives. Perhaps we have been to communal celebrations of the sacrament of penance, witnessed the ordination of an acquaintance to the priesthood, or been present when a loved one was anointed. These events are liturgical acts where Christ is truly present in a unique way. They are also special times of prayer. We are called, as Catholics, to be attentive to the spiritual realities

made present by the signs and to participate actively at each celebration of the sacraments. We are never mere observers.

We may attend a wedding because we are invited and because
we want to share our friends' joy. But we are also privileged to
pray for those friends, and our active participation can help open
them to God's blessings. We may be present at a funeral out of
respect for the deceased and to show our love for the family. But
as Catholics we pray for the deceased, and our prayers can help
escort the deceased to the happiness of heaven. At baptisms and
confirmations, we pray that those receiving these sacraments may
be open to the grace Jesus offers, not only as the water is poured
or the oil bestowed, but always. At communal penance services,
we pray for pardon and peace for ourselves and the whole Church.
At ordinations, we attend as members of the Church calling the
new deacon or priest or bishop to be faithful to the holy order
bestowed by Jesus. At an anointing of the sick, we are there
to bring the sick person to Christ, in imitation of those in the
gospels who brought friends to him (Mark 1:32–34; 2:1–12). At
each celebration of the sacraments, we are present as members
of Christ's body. Through us Jesus is present. We offer our lives
and prayers in union with his.

BENEDICTION AND ADORATION
OF THE BLESSED SACRAMENT

Christ's real presence in the Eucharist derives from the fact that
at Mass he changes bread and wine into his body and blood. For
this reason, the Catholic Church preserves the Blessed Sacrament
in churches or chapels so holy Communion may be available to
the sick, and the faithful may adore Christ in the Eucharist.

The Church highly recommends public and private devotion
to the Blessed Sacrament outside Mass. All such devotion should
always be closely linked to the Mass, as Pope John Paul II affirmed
in his encyclical letter, On the Eucharist in Its Relationship to the

Church (*Ecclesia de Eucharistia*, 25). The most common public devotion is exposition of the Blessed Sacrament with Benediction, an act of liturgical worship. The consecrated host is placed on the altar in a monstrance (a sacred vessel in which the host may be seen). The Scriptures are read, prayers are said, hymns are sung, and some time is devoted to silent prayer. Adoration may be expressed by the use of incense. Then the congregation is blessed with the holy Eucharist, and the liturgical service concludes with prayers and a hymn. This devotion, of course, is a clear demonstration of our faith in the real presence, and it nourishes and strengthens that faith.

Many Catholic parishes have instituted the practice of perpetual adoration, where members of the faithful maintain a constant presence before the Blessed Sacrament exposed on the altar. Other parishes set aside a day or two each week for adoration. From such eucharistic adoration flow many benefits, including vocations to the priesthood and religious life, new appreciation of the sacrament of matrimony, and greater concern for charity and justice.

Catholics are also encouraged to make visits to the Blessed Sacrament. Some people drop in at Catholic churches frequently just to "say hello to the Lord." Some have the practice of making a holy hour, spending time in the Lord's presence.

What might we do in such an hour of prayer? First, there should be time to enjoy being with Jesus, to talk with him about family, work, and what is happening in our lives. This may lead to quiet contemplation before the Lord. Betty describes how God spoke to her heart during an hour of adoration:

As I came into the chapel, I knelt and prayed to God about things going on in my life with my children, family, and others. When I sat and picked up my prayer book the words, "Be still, and know that I am God!" (Psalm 46:10), came to mind. Well, on that day being still was the last thing on the agenda. But as I sat there in the silence and repeated, "Be still, and know that I am God," the peace was overwhelming. My busy life and things I had no control over (but wanted to) all seemed to fade away. In my heart I knew God was in control, even though I did not understand his plan. That was one short hour! It was over before I knew it, and my prayer book was still unopened. When things get crazy, I think back on that day and repeat to myself, "Be still, and know that I am God." And then I pray, "Yes Lord, you are God. Help me to turn this over to you and trust in you."

While adoring the Blessed Sacrament, we can receive spiritual communion—inviting Jesus to live in our hearts when we cannot receive him sacramentally. We can reflect on Scripture, especially those passages used at the Sunday Masses, an excellent way to relate our time of adoration to the Eucharist. We may offer prayers in the words of Scripture, in formulas found in prayer books, or in popular prayers such as the rosary. We might read from a good Catholic book, pausing to talk to Jesus about thoughts that touch our hearts. If we get into the habit of making an hour of adoration before Jesus, we will find that time goes by too quickly, as it does in the presence of any good friend.

THE LITURGY OF THE HOURS

Catholics believe that we find God in the everyday deeds and hourly routines that make up our lives. From New Testament times the Church has exemplified this reality by recommending that we unite ordinary actions to God in patterns of prayer. The New Testament speaks of the apostles praying at various times (Acts 1:12–15; 3:1; 10:9; 16:25), and gradually the Church came to celebrate prayer throughout the day in the Liturgy of the Hours, also called the Divine Office.

As now prayed by priests, deacons, religious, and many laypeople, the Liturgy of the Hours consists of five "hours" or times for prayer. These are Office of Readings, Morning Prayer, Midday Prayer, Evening Prayer, and Night Prayer. Each includes psalms, Scripture readings, and intercessions. Variety is provided by a four-week cycle of the hours, as well as by a calendar of feasts that follows the Church year.

The *Catechism of the Catholic Church* points out that the Liturgy of the Hours is so devised that it sanctifies the whole course of day and night.

In this "public prayer of the Church," the faithful (clergy, religious, and lay people) exercise the royal priesthood of the baptized. Celebrated in "the form approved" by the Church, the Liturgy of the Hours "is truly the voice of the Bride herself addressed to her Bridegroom. It is the very prayer which Christ himself together with his Body addresses to the Father (1174).

The *Catechism* adds: "The Liturgy of the Hours is intended to become the prayer of the whole People of God....The laity, too, are encouraged to recite the divine office, either with the priests, or among themselves, or even individually" (1175). So the Liturgy of the Hours is liturgical prayer for all Catholics. It has become increasingly popular in recent years. Some parishes invite members to communal recitation of parts of the Liturgy of the Hours, especially morning and evening prayer. Some laypeople recite the entire Office each day, and others recite one or another part. Anyone may obtain the entire four-volume set of the *Liturgy of the Hours,* or an abbreviated version, at Catholic bookstores.

One feature of the Liturgy of the Hours deserving of attention is its frequent use of the Book of Psalms. We studied the psalms in Chapter Two, and you may wish to review the explanation of

Hebrew poetry given there. The Liturgy of the Hours has greater meaning for us when we understand the poetry of the psalms and something about their background. Also, the realization that saying the Liturgy of the Hours joins us to believers who have prayed the psalms for over three millennia can encourage us as we pray.

I'd like to emphasize the importance of applying each psalm to our own life situation or to those of others. When we pray a psalm for a person who is experiencing some need described in a particular psalm, our prayer reaches out to others. As intercession, our prayer in yet another way becomes the prayer of the Church, and of Jesus as he continues to intercede for his Church.

THE BOOK OF BLESSINGS

The *Book of Blessings*, part of the Church's liturgy, is a fine resource for Catholic prayer. Some blessings, like those of religious articles and those connected to a church function, must be celebrated by a bishop, priest, or deacon. But most liturgical blessings may be given by any Catholic.

Liturgical blessings follow a typical pattern. After a brief introduction and opening prayer, there is a reading from sacred Scripture followed by a responsorial psalm. Next come intercessions, to which may be added special intentions of the participants and recitation of the Lord's Prayer. The prayer of blessing is then said, accompanied by some outward sign such as the raising of hands, the laying on of hands, the Sign of the Cross, sprinkling with holy water, or the use of incense. The liturgy closes with a brief concluding rite.

This structure allows those present to participate. In a family blessing of a Christmas tree, for example, the father might give the introduction and proclaim the readings, the children offer the intercessions, and the mother could say the blessing. In most cases, there are alternate short blessing forms available, but even in their longer forms the prayers of blessing take only a few minutes and are so designed that small children can be involved.

There are two English editions of the *Book of Blessings* approved for use in the United States. The first contains all the liturgical blessings of the Church. The second is a shorter edition that is more suitable for laypeople. It can be obtained at most Catholic bookstores, and it should find an honored place in every Catholic home.

BECOMING FAMILIAR WITH THE BOOK OF BLESSINGS

The *Shorter Book of Blessings* begins with a general introduction that offers a fine explanation of blessing prayers in the history of salvation. It explains that blessings "are signs that have God's word as their basis and are celebrated from motives of faith... signs above all of spiritual effects that are achieved through the Church's intercession" (p. 22, #10). It indicates that the purpose of all blessings is to sanctify people, to help them grow in holiness and in their ability to serve God.

Part One, the first main division of the book, contains blessings pertaining to persons. Here are found blessings of families, of engaged and married couples, of children, of parents before and after childbirth, of those celebrating a birthday, of the elderly, of the sick, of students and teachers, and of travelers. There are special blessings for particular circumstances, such as blessings for parents after a miscarriage, parents of an adopted child, people suffering from addiction or substance abuse, and victims of crime.

Part Two has blessings related to buildings and to various forms of human activity. There are blessings for homes and other structures, for automobiles, boats and fishing gear, for tools and equipment, for animals, for fields and flocks, for planting and harvest, and for athletic events. There are several forms of blessings to be used before and after meals.

Part Three includes blessings for religious articles such as rosaries, scapulars, and medals. These must be offered by a priest or deacon.

Part Four contains blessings related to feasts and seasons. Some, like blessings for Advent wreaths, Nativity scenes, and Christmas trees, are especially suitable for family celebrations. There are blessings of homes at Christmas and Easter, of throats for Saint Blaise Day, of ashes for Ash Wednesday, of food for special occasions, of mothers for Mother's Day, and of fathers for Father's Day. There is also a rite of blessing for visiting cemeteries on All Souls' Day, Memorial Day, and anniversaries.

Part Five contains blessings said by a priest or deacon for parish council members and officers of parish societies. There are blessings for inaugurating public officials. There are general blessings for giving thanks and for asking God to bless people, things, and events not specifically mentioned elsewhere.

Finally, there is an appendix with solemn blessings and prayers over the people. These, taken from the *Roman Missal,* may be used to conclude other blessings, or on any occasion when a priest or deacon is asked to give a blessing.

BLESSINGS ARE A BLESSING

Most Catholics make the Sign of the Cross and say the traditional "Bless us, O Lord, and these thy gifts..." before meals. But they may not be aware of their right from baptism and confirmation to offer other blessings.

Carol Ann started blessing her children every night when they were small. This became a family tradition that expanded to include friends (even of college age!) who also wanted to be blessed. The custom has continued now that the children have grown up, with family members often saying prayers of blessing for one another. They feel that their prayers of blessing have been life-transforming.

Hopefully, many Catholics will imitate Carol Ann and her family in the frequent use of the *Shorter Book of Blessings*. The book's riches can only be hinted at in this brief summary, but Catholics who use it regularly will enhance their prayer life and grow closer to the God of all blessings.

SACRAMENTAL OBJECTS

Jesus gave his Church the sacraments, outward signs of inward grace. The water of baptism, the oil of confirmation and anointing of the sick, the bread and wine of the Eucharist, and all the other signs of the sacraments inspired the Church to appreciate the goodness of material things and their ability to signify spiritual realities. As a consequence, the Church has designated many other signs as *sacramentals,* blessed objects that bear some resemblance to the sacraments and bring graces obtained through the intercession of the Church.

Sacramentals are closely related to the sacraments. When, for example, we dip our fingers in holy water and make the Sign of the Cross, we are reminded of our baptism in the name of the Father, Son, and Holy Spirit. At the Easter Vigil, a large candle is lit to symbolize Christ's resurrection from the darkness of the grave. At every baptism, a blessed candle is lit from the paschal candle to symbolize that Christ's life and light are granted to the baptized.

Blessed candles and votive lights are related to the Eucharist as well as to baptism, reminding us that Christ is "the light of the world" (John 8:12). Crosses, crucifixes, and the Stations of the Cross call to mind the saving death of Christ made present in the Eucharist. On Passion Sunday, palms are blessed at a celebration of the Eucharist; they remind us of Christ's willingness to accept death on the cross to save us. I heard a true story about a priest who told the congregation that women of the parish had woven palm crosses. He wanted to give a cross to every family in the parish. He advised, "I'd like you to place this cross in the room where you have the most arguments. The cross will remind you that Jesus died to bring forgiveness and peace." After the service, a woman walked up to the priest, introduced herself, and said, "I'll take five of those crosses!"

On Ash Wednesday, palms from the previous year are burned; the ashes are then blessed and used to sign the faithful in the form of a cross as a call to repentance. This signing with blessed ashes is related to the sacrament of penance.

Wedding rings, which are blessed and exchanged at Catholic weddings, are sacramentals, signs of love and commitment. Being made of precious metal, they are reminders of the infinite value of God's love. Being circular in form, they show that human love originates in God's love that has existed from all eternity and will endure forever.

Other sacramentals, such as rosaries, medals, statues, and sacred images, are at least implicitly connected to the sacraments, for they remind us of the supernatural life given us by Jesus. The rosary unites us to Mary, who lived in the grace of her Son and who now watches over us, her children. Medals, statues, and sacred images direct our attention to the saints who model fidelity to the grace given at baptism. These, and all sacramentals, dispose us to "receive the chief effect of the sacraments, and various occasions in life are rendered holy" by their use (CCC 1667).

Making Use of Sacramentals

Blessings and sacramentals are elements of Catholicism that have their foundation in Scripture. Jesus blessed people and things. He used mud and saliva to cure a blind man (John 9:6), and he instructed his apostles to anoint the sick with oil. The Acts of the Apostles describes how the first Christians used signs to bring Christ's healing to people: "God did extraordinary miracles through Paul, so that when the handkerchiefs or aprons that had touched his skin were brought to the sick, their diseases left them, and the evil spirits came out of them" (Acts 19:11–12).

Inspired by Jesus and the testimony of Scripture, the Church has recommended the use of sacramentals as signs of God's care for us. Catholics have embraced the sacramentals with enthusiasm because they fit into our natural inclination to use material things as symbols of profound realities. Gifts are signs that convey love and help love grow. Works of art can express powerful emotions and elicit them from people who experience the art. So, too, the sacramentals express God's generosity and power and open us to God's grace.

In today's world, where materialism flourishes, sacramentals declare the importance of spiritual realities and the life of prayer. Medals, crucifixes, and statues remind us of God's presence and prompt us to pray. Holy water, blessed candles, and other sacramentals are prayers in action. Sprinkling holy water on a person or object is a prayer, with or without words. A burning candle symbolizes prayer. When I was a small child, my mother used to light a blessed candle in threatening weather. We would pray, and this never failed to bring comfort and courage.

I once read about a mother who took her small children to a beautiful cathedral. They were in awe of everything, but were especially interested in the vigil candles burning before an altar. The mother explained how the candles express petitions to God. She placed an offering in the collection box, then told the children that each could light a candle while mentioning a special need to God. When they finished, she asked if there were any questions. The smallest girl replied, "No questions. But if there's a pony on the steps outside, it's mine!"

We began this reflection on liturgical prayer by referring to Jesus' sense of humor. We close with a true children's story that should bring a smile. And why not? Prayer, especially liturgical prayer, brings joy. The psalmist says to God: "You show me the path of life. / In your presence there is fullness of joy" (Psalm 16:11).

QUESTIONS FOR
DISCUSSION AND REFLECTION

Did you know that laypeople can give blessings? Were you aware that families could offer liturgical prayer (the official prayer of the Church) in their homes? What are the ways this can be done?

Have you ever used the *Book of Blessings?* If so, which blessings have you used? If not, is this kind of liturgical prayer of interest to you? What does the Church say is the special value of prayer in the *Book of Blessings?*

What is your fondest memory of the use of sacramentals when you were a child? What is your favorite sacramental today?

ACTIVITIES

Go through various parts of the Mass and discover the many ACTS of prayer found in them. For example, the *Gloria* adores God ("we worship...we praise you"), asks pardon ("have mercy on us"), thanks God ("we give you thanks"), and makes requests ("receive our prayer").

The next time you are in the presence of the Blessed Sacrament, read and pray Psalm 84. Ask Jesus to give you the love and devotion for God's dwelling place expressed in this beautiful psalm.

Chapter Seven

THE BIBLE TRANSLATED
INTO PRAYER

꧁ ༷ ꧂

In a discussion on prayer, Father Jacob described the rosary as "the Bible translated into prayer." The rosary takes the great mysteries of the Bible from the printed page and writes them on our hearts. This calls to mind the new covenant foretold by Jeremiah when God promised, "I will put my law within them, and I will write it on their hearts; and I will be their God, and they shall be my people" (Jeremiah 31:33).

Through the rosary, God's word is written on our hearts as we pray in the company of Mary, the Mother of Jesus. In the New Testament, Mary is the model believer, one who treasures the words and actions of Jesus, "all these things in her heart" (Luke 2:51). In her company and that of all the saints and angels, the Bible is translated into prayer.

Devotion to saints and angels and prayer with them are important elements of Catholicism, gifts we accept joyfully from God and share with others. A proper understanding of these gifts begins, fittingly, in the Bible.

JESUS, SAINTS, AND ANGELS

I've often been asked by Christians who are not Catholic about our devotion to the saints. Some Christians say we should pray only to God. Others suppose that those in heaven are not aware of what happens on earth. In response, I go directly to Jesus, who teaches devotion to the saints by his life and example. Jesus spoke to saints who had died long before his birth. Jesus received help from residents of heaven. Jesus delegated residents of heaven to speak for him.

When Jesus was making his journey to Jerusalem and the cross, he forewarned his apostles about his passion and death. They did not understand. But heavenly visitors did. On the Mount of Transfiguration, Moses and Elijah came to Jesus. "They appeared in glory and were speaking of his departure, which he was about to accomplish at Jerusalem" (Luke 9:31). When Jesus endured such agony in the Garden of Gethsemane that he sweated blood, "an angel from heaven appeared to him and gave him strength" (Luke 22:43). Jesus himself talked with saints and angels in prayers, and when we do so, we follow his example. Jesus received help from saints and angels. When we seek assistance from them, we imitate Jesus.

Scripture tells us that at the death of Jesus, "many bodies of the saints who had fallen asleep were raised. After his resurrection they came out of the tombs and entered the holy city and appeared to many" (Matthew 27:52–53). Jesus could have appeared to those people himself, but instead he delegated saints to spread the good news of his resurrection. Heaven is not a place of silent slumber, but of joyous activity in the service of God. Angels who see God's face in heaven watch over and guard us (Matthew 18:10). The saints delight in carrying out God's will and assisting us on earth. We delight in receiving their assistance.

HONORING THE SAINTS

It is clear from the life of Jesus that angels and saints in heaven know what is happening on earth and want to help us. We respond to their assistance by honoring them as does God's inspired Word. The Book of Revelation proclaims, "Blessed are the dead who from now on die in the Lord" (14:13). The honor paid the saints in heaven is symbolized by their white linen robes that represent "the righteous deeds of the saints" (Revelation 19:8).

Catholic devotion to the saints often involves the use of statues and other sacred images. Some people think these are forbidden by the Bible. Not at all. God gave Moses the commandment: "I am the LORD your God....You shall not make for yourself an idol..." (Exodus 20:4–5). God forbade the making of *idols* (representations of false gods), not of statues or other carved images. Exodus 25:18–22 relates how God commanded Moses to make two cherubim (carvings of angelic guardians) and to place them above the Ark of the Covenant. The Book of Numbers (21:4–9) says that when the Israelites sinned against God and were being tormented by saraph (venomous) serpents, God told Moses to make an image of a snake and put it on a pole. All who looked at the snake would be healed. Statues and carvings of cherubim, palm trees, flowers, oxen, lions, and cherubim were placed in Solomon's temple in Jerusalem (1 Kings 6:23–30; 7:23–29). The Bible says God was pleased with the temple and all its details, and dwelt there (1 Kings 8).

God likes statues! So should we. They help us remember the saints, as the Bible teaches: "Remember your leaders, those who spoke the word of God to you; consider the outcome of their way of life and imitate their faith" (Hebrews 13:7). God honors heroes and heroines in the Bible, sometimes with entire books, as in the Books of Ruth, Judith, and Esther. We follow God's lead when we honor and memorialize the saints in stone and stained glass.

In America we have statues of great heroes in public buildings. Most people have pictures of relatives in their homes. If the Bible forbade the making of all images, then such statues and pictures would be forbidden. Further, many Christians erect statues of Mary, Joseph, and Jesus at Christmas when they put up manger scenes. Just as statues of George Washington and Abraham Lincoln remind us of their great lives; just as pictures of relatives remind us of their love; just as manger scenes remind us of Jesus, Mary, and Joseph; so statues of the saints remind us of how they loved Jesus and achieved greatness through his grace. Statues of the saints encourage us to imitate their holiness and to pray for their help.

Sometimes there is confusion about Catholic use of statues and devotion to the saints. A couple in southeast Missouri told me that their son Nathan brought home a note from his teacher which read, "Dear parents, today, September 8, is the birthday of the Blessed Virgin Mary, and we celebrated with a birthday party. The kids really enjoyed it, so be sure to ask them about it. Mrs. Shaffer." The mother continued, "I asked Nathan. 'Did you do anything special at school today?'" He said, "Oh yeah, we had a birthday party." I inquired, "Whom was it for?" Nathan replied, "Mrs. Shaffer's statue."

Of course, the party was for Mary, not the statue! Catholics do not pray to statues or venerate them. We pray to and venerate the saints. But a further distinction is in order. Our veneration of Mary and the saints is not *worship*. Worship is the adoration due to God alone—Father, Son, and Holy Spirit. The *Catechism* says clearly that our devotion to Mary "differs essentially from the adoration which is given to the incarnate Word and equally to the Father and the Holy Spirit, and greatly fosters this adoration" (971).

We Catholics must be aware of what the Church really teaches about devotion to the saints and about how such devotion actually nourishes our worship of God. In religion classes, I have often placed this statement on tests: "True or False—Catholics do not worship statues, but the saints represented by the statues." We do not worship the statues or the saints. We worship God alone, and in this worship we are joined by the saints who continually adore God in heaven.

PRAYING TO THE SAINTS

Catholics are sometimes asked why we pray to the saints instead of going directly to God. We do go directly to God, but we also pray to the saints. We should note that we do not pray to God and to the saints in the same way. We pray to God as the source of all blessings. We pray to the saints in the sense that we ask them to pray with us and for us, and to lead us closer to God. This is illustrated in two prayers said often by Catholics. In the Lord's Prayer, we ask God to do what only God can do: "Give us this day our daily bread, and forgive us our trespasses." In the Hail Mary, we ask Mary to "pray for us sinners."

Scripture shows that those in heaven pray for us. The Book of Revelation pictures those in heaven offering to God the prayers of God's people on earth (called "saints" in the *New Revised Standard Version*): "...the twenty-four elders fell before the Lamb, each holding a harp and golden bowls full of incense, which are the prayers of the saints" (5:8). The Second Book of Maccabees (15:12–15) reports a vision in which the martyred high priest Onias and the prophet Jeremiah pray for the Jewish nation. This demonstrates the Jewish belief that saints pray for us, a belief that Jesus and the first Christians took for granted. If we want to imitate the first Christians, we honor the saints and pray to them.

But why pray to the saints at all? Some people suppose that we must convince God to do what is best for us, and the more advocates arguing our case the better. But this is not so. God knows what is best for us and wants to do what is best. God does not need to be convinced.

Others think that the saints, especially Mary, will do favors when God isn't interested. When Lou Holtz was football coach at Notre Dame University, he was interviewed by a writer from a national sports magazine. The writer said, "Lou, I've heard

that you and your team pray before every game." "That's right,"
Lou replied. The writer continued, "You don't think God cares
whether Notre Dame wins or not, do you?" "No," Lou said with
a grin, "God doesn't care....But his Mother does!"

That's a true story, and a funny one. I'm sure Lou was just
kidding, because it's bad theology. Mary and the saints don't
step in where God is unwilling. But that still leaves the question,
"Why pray to the saints?"

The answer lies in the importance of prayer *with* others and
for others. Jesus teaches the special value of praying with others:
"Where two or three are gathered in my name, I am there among
them" (Matthew 18:20). Saint Paul asked believers to pray for
him (Colossians 4:3; 1 Thessalonians 5:25) because he felt it
was important to have others praying with him and for him. It
is good to pray with those on earth and ask them to pray for us.
It is even better to pray with the saints in heaven and ask them to
pray for us. Why? Not because prayer changes God, but because
prayer changes us.

Consider the case of two little boys with the same illness in
adjoining hospital rooms. Both receive exactly the same medical
treatment. But one is from a dysfunctional family. He is alone,
with no visitors and no encouragement from relatives or friends.
The other comes from a caring family. A parent is always in the
room. There are visitors, balloons at the bedside table, and greet-
ing cards in the mail. The boy from the caring family is certain
to recover more quickly because his family's love conditions him
to receive all the healing doctors can give. So too, the knowledge
that we are supported by a heavenly family opens us to all God
can do for us.

THE COMMUNION OF SAINTS

The Bible shows that we have a heavenly community, communion with the saints. We are "citizens with the saints and also members of the household of God, built upon the foundation of the apostles and prophets, with Christ Jesus himself as the cornerstone" (Ephesians 2:19–20). Scripture reveals that the saints in heaven know what happens here on earth. Jesus speaks of the "joy in heaven over one sinner who repents" (Luke 15:7). The Letter to the Hebrews compares life to a race, and portrays the saints, victors from the past, as witnesses of our efforts. They cheer us on as we run the race of life. "Therefore, since we are surrounded by so great a cloud of witnesses, let us...run with perseverance the race that is set before us, looking to Jesus the pioneer and perfecter of our faith" (12:1–2).

Catholics believe, then, in the communion of saints, the company of those united in Christ on earth, in purgatory, and heaven. The communion of saints has been described with some humor as "all saints, all souls, and all sorts." We are "all sorts" of people here on earth who hope to join the saints in heaven. We believe that it is God's plan to "gather up all things in him, things in heaven and things on earth" (Ephesians 1:10), to bring about a community of love and prayer among those in this world and the next.

Community is essential to us as human beings. Companions—relatives and friends—are blessings that bring comfort and happiness. They share our joys and help us endure sufferings. This community does not cease when loved ones move into eternity. We know this from Scripture, from passages already cited and from others, like Jesus' parable of the vine and branches (John 15:1–6). Danny, who grew up in a family of thirteen, wrote:

Family peace and cohesiveness are graces from heaven. I remember my mother's nightly rounds of bedtime prayers, one for each child, bed to bed to bed. I heard a chorus of "Amen" and "Alleluia" in one room, "Sing a New Song" in the next. There was always an assumption among us that we prayed as a group, holding hands when possible, especially where beds were huddled in small rooms. Not unlike the popular television show of the time, *The Waltons*, we sang our goodnight out loud, naming names and praising God: "Good night, Eileen; Good night, Ann; Good night, Joe....Amen, Alleluia." I took great pride in the size of our family and the connection we shared. The validity of our faith was never more tested than during the months and years following the deaths of two of my siblings, Ken and Ruth. Despite tragic circumstances, I never felt separated from my fallen brother and sister. Oddly, I began to see them in new, deep, and profound ways. I wanted to call out to them during prayer time and to hold their hands. My mother comforted me with the parable of the vine and the branches. "We are connected to Jesus like branches on a vine," she said. "He is the Vine and we are the branches. Just as we reach out and pray our 'Amen' hand to hand in the bedroom (like branches connected to the Vine), so, too, we touch our kin in heaven who are connected to the same Vine." From that day forward the communion of saints has profoundly changed my perception of life, death, and new life. I feel connected to all my family through Jesus. I have eternal companions for prayer, and my hand is always held by another. Good night, Ken. Good night, Ruth. Tomorrow we rise again.

ALL SAINTS

Danny's story reminds us that there are many saints in heaven who are not officially canonized. The Church acknowledges this every year on November 1 by observing the Solemnity of All Saints. We should honor all the saints, especially our own saints, friends, and family members, and ask them for their intercession and help. Father Art, a priest for more than fifty years, says, "I have a single-spaced page of names of my saints. I take out the list, talk with them, and ask for their prayers."

Each of us can remember people who never made the headlines, but lived holy lives, loved Jesus, and served others with kindness and generosity. I have known many such saints, and I often turn to them for help. In the lives of these saints, we find courage and strength. We discover patterns of living that guide us to the eternal happiness they now enjoy.

Thanks to the communion of saints, we can do more than remember the saints. We live in their company. We visit them in spirit. We communicate with them in prayer. An elderly gentleman observed with a smile, "Before my wife died, we used to go dancing a lot. Now we just talk."

WAYS OF PRAYING WITH THE SAINTS

There are as many ways of praying with the saints as there are ways of prayer. We may use any form of vocal prayer in speaking to the saints. At every Mass we ask the intercession of the saints. The Bible offers prayers sung by the saints in heaven (Revelation 4:11), and affirms that we on earth pray with those in heaven (Revelation 5:13). We may talk to the saints in our own words. We may use prayer formulas like the Hail Mary and *Memorare*, or other prayers to Mary and the saints.

A well-known form of vocal prayer to the saints is the litany.

Litanies may be said as private or common prayer. In community, a leader speaks or sings a series of petitions or invocations (such as a list of saints or of titles for Mary), and people answer with a set response like "pray for us." The Litany of the Saints, used in some liturgical services, calls on many saints by name to pray for us, and lists our needs and requests. Other litanies have been approved by the Church for public use, most notably the Litany of Loreto of the Blessed Virgin Mary.

Whether said in community or in private, litanies offer an opportunity to reflect on spiritual realities while we recite the vocal prayers. We may consider virtues of the saints whose names are mentioned, or we may let Mary's titles in the Litany of Loreto encourage us to imitate her virtues. We should not just rush through the prayers. An extreme (and perhaps fictional) example is that of a lady who was assigned the Litany of the Saints as a penance. A gentleman praying nearby in the quiet church heard her say: "All the saints on the first page, pray for us. All the saints on the second page, intercede for us. All the saints on the third page, hear our prayer. From all the things on the last page, deliver us, O Lord." Real prayer involves mind and heart, not just the recitation of words.

The rosary deserves special note because of its popularity. It combines vocal prayer with meditation, showing that prayer is a matter of body and spirit. The rosary, with its cross, chain, and beads, is something we can see and touch. The vocal prayers of the rosary involve our voice and hearing. The words remind us that Mary and the saints are one with us in prayer. The mysteries of the rosary do indeed translate the Bible into prayer. They bind our lives to the historical life of Christ and foreshadow our eternal destiny, union with Christ in heaven. (For a more complete explanation of the rosary with meditations on each of the twenty mysteries, patterns for applying the mysteries to our own life, and suggestions for using them as intercessory prayer, see my book, *Christ's Mother and Ours*).

Our Catholic practice of honoring patron saints, those whose names are given at baptism, encourages us to turn to these saints as models of holiness and prayer. We pray to them, and as the *Catechism* indicates, they pray for us. "The patron saint provides a model of charity and the assurance of his prayer" (2165).

PRAYING FOR THE SOULS IN PURGATORY

The Bible teaches that it is "holy and pious" to pray for the dead (2 Maccabees 12:45). Martyrs and great saints enter heaven at death. Those who have rejected God by unrepented mortal sin choose hell as their eternal destiny. Those in heaven do not need prayer, and those in hell are beyond the reach of prayer. But some people die neither perfectly ready for heaven nor completely alienated from God. Such persons need purification to achieve the holiness required to stand in God's presence, where "nothing unclean will enter" (Revelation 21:27). This state of purification is called *purgatory*. Catholics have always prayed for the souls in purgatory, helping them on their journey to eternal bliss. And we believe that their prayers help us.

The Church bases belief in purgatory on the biblical teaching of prayer for the dead, which goes back to Old Testament times. Some Jewish soldiers, fighting for freedom under the great patriot, Judas Maccabeus, had been slain. They were found to be wearing pagan amulets, a practice forbidden by Jewish law. Their comrades prayed for the dead that the sinful deed might be blotted out. Then Judas took up a collection—which he sent to Jerusalem to provide for an expiatory sacrifice. The Bible comments that this was holy and pious, and affirms that Judas made atonement for the dead that they might be freed from this sin (2 Maccabees 12:43–45). If heaven and hell were the only possibilities after death, there would be no reason to pray for the dead. As a result, the Church reasoned to the existence of purgatory, an intermediate state where people can be helped by prayer.

Several New Testament passages also point to the existence of purgatory. In the First Letter to the Corinthians (3:13–15), Paul refers to a day of judgment and a testing by fire that fits the traditional doctrine of purgatory. In the Second Letter to Timothy (1:16–18), Paul offers a prayer asking mercy for a faithful Christian who had died.

Inspired by these passages, believers have prayed for their beloved dead from New Testament times, as evidenced by inscriptions in early Christian burial places. In the fourth century, Saint Monica made the deathbed request of her son, Saint Augustine, that he remember her at the altar of the Lord. Augustine witnessed to the fact that early Christians prayed for the dead and relied on the prayer of the saints. He said that we pray for those who have died, but not the martyrs. Instead, they pray for us, that we may follow in their footsteps (*Treatise on John*, Tract 84:1–2; *The Liturgy of the Hours*, II, 450).

To understand the doctrine of purgatory and prayer for those in purgatory, we must distinguish between what Jesus has done and what we must do. Christ has done everything necessary for our salvation, but he does not force salvation on us. Rather, he invites us to accept it with a living faith and a love like his own (John 13:34). The only suitable response to the love of a Savior who gave his life on the cross for us is a love that strives to match his. But we so often fall short. Christ offers us an ocean of grace, and we come to him with a thimble. God gives us our time on earth so that we may open mind, will, and heart to Christ's truth and love, and we fail to do all we should to reach this goal.

If we die in a state of imperfection, neither estranged from God by unrepented mortal sin, nor perfectly attuned to God's goodness and love, we will not be ready for heaven. To fully enjoy God's presence, we must have our abilities to know and love at the peak of perfection. If we were to go sightseeing at the Grand Canyon and discover that our sunglasses were dirty, we'd want to clean them. Before we enter heaven, we will want to fine-tune our mind, will, and heart so that we can fully enjoy the beauty, truth, and love of God. Purgatory is God's gift making this possible. And thanks to the communion of saints, we will not be alone. We will be helped by the prayers of friends on earth and friends in heaven.

Popular explanations of purgatory in the past have sometimes included graphic descriptions of the suffering of the "poor souls." However, those in purgatory are assured of heaven and are closer to the love of God than we are on earth. As a result, they experience profound joy. At the same time they have a clear realization of the evil of even the smallest sin. They suffer the pain of knowing they are not yet ready to enter the joys of heaven. Their purification comes, not from physical fire, but from the fire of God's love. "For...our God is a consuming fire" (Hebrews 12:29). Just as fire burns away impurities when gold is refined, so God's love will burn away imperfections and raise human capabilities to their utmost. Our prayers and those of the saints help open the souls in purgatory to all God's love can do.

We do not know who might need purgatory, and since those in purgatory are beyond Earth's space and time, it is not possible to know how long anyone might be there. But God is not limited by time. We may pray as long as we wish for our beloved dead. God can take our prayers of a lifetime and apply them when they are needed. It is, as Scripture says, "holy and pious" to pray for the dead.

THE BIBLE TRANSLATED INTO LIFE

The rosary, as mentioned at the beginning of this chapter, translates the Bible into prayer. The saints do even more. They teach us by their lives on earth how to reach the joys of heaven. As we ponder their example, as we enjoy union with them and with the souls in purgatory, we are encouraged to continue our journey to eternal life. We hear "every creature in heaven and on earth...

singing, / 'To the one seated on the throne and to the Lamb / be blessing and honor and glory and might / forever and ever!'" (Revelation 5:13). The rosary translates the Bible into prayer. The saints translate the Bible into prayer, and into life!

QUESTIONS FOR DISCUSSION AND REFLECTION

How would you explain why Catholics honor the saints and pray to the saints? Who is your favorite saint, the one you turn to most often in prayer? How often do you pray to your guardian angel? To your patron saints?

Father Art has made a list of the saints he has known, friends and family members who have touched him and whom he asks for help. Have you ever made such a list?

ACTIVITIES

Find a quiet place and take a few minutes to think about family and friends who have gone before you and touched you by their holiness of life. Thank God for their goodness. Ask them to pray for you, that you may one day join them in heaven.

Remember loved ones who have died. Pray for the repose of their souls. You may wish to use this traditional prayer: "Eternal rest give unto them, O Lord, and let perpetual light shine upon them. May their souls and the souls of the faithful departed, through the mercy of God, rest in peace. Amen."

Chapter Eight

DIFFICULTIES IN PRAYER

∽⫶∾

D ifficulties in prayer are common, even among the saints. Saint Teresa of Ávila is said to have endured a period of many years when she said talking to God was like talking to a stone wall. Saint Pio of Pietrelcina (Padre Pio), who had many mystical experiences, was a down-to-earth man who was sympathetic to those whose prayers seemed to go unanswered. He told the story of a priest who was asked by a farmer to pray for the recovery of a sick cow. At the intercessions, the priest said loudly, "That this good farmer's cow may die, we pray to the Lord." At the end of the Mass, the farmer went up to the priest and complained. The priest assured him, "Don't worry. Your cow will be fine. The Lord always does the opposite of what I ask!"

If saints can have difficulties in prayer, we should not be surprised that we do, too. This chapter addresses some of those difficulties. Most were presented to me as questions from students of Catholic Home Study Service, a ministry I've been directing since 1991. Others are questions asked at classes or parish missions.

DISTRACTIONS

Perhaps the most common difficulty in prayer is dealing with distractions. One young woman wrote, "I find prayer very difficult. My mind is always filled with thousands of details that I can't seem to get rid of when I try to quiet down to pray. Do you have any suggestions for me?" An elderly lady asked, "What's wrong with me? My mind wanders when I try to pray."

I told the elderly lady, "A mind that wanders when we try to pray doesn't mean that something is wrong with us. It means that we are human." And the very fact that we are concerned about distractions shows that we want to pray well. God is certainly pleased with our desire to pray more fervently.

Most of us have to battle distractions in prayer. Our minds move quickly from one thing to another. This doesn't mean that we should resign ourselves to mediocre attempts at communicating with God. Prayer is like most other human endeavors. The more effort we put into it, the more likely we are to succeed. But because we are human we can expect imperfections, and we should not be discouraged if distractions come despite our best efforts.

Where to begin? We should build our prayer life on the solid foundation of the Church's teaching, which is based on the wisdom and life of Jesus and summarized in the *Catechism of the Catholic Church*. As we do this, we will become aware of the many possibilities for prayer in our Catholic tradition. In this book, we have studied that tradition and the many ways of prayer available to us. The more we know about these ways of prayer and the more we learn how to use them, the better we will be able to ward off distractions.

MINIMIZING DISTRACTIONS

We can minimize distractions in our private prayer by setting aside a special place and time for prayer, as previously suggested. In liturgical prayer, we can avoid many distractions with a little preparation. If we habitually rush into church at the last minute, it can be very difficult to recollect ourselves for Mass. We should try to arrive early and spend five or ten minutes before Mass thinking of the great miracle about to take place. We can pray for the celebrant, for others who will be leading the liturgy, and for the members of the congregation, especially those burdened by trials or suffering. We can meditate on the Scripture readings for the day. We can recall how Jesus will be present to us in the gathering of the community, in the prayers and readings, and above all in the Eucharist.

OVERCOMING DISTRACTIONS

When distractions come, we may find it better to sidestep them than to battle them head-on or fret about them. When we notice a distraction, we should gently turn our attention back to God. We may have to do this often during a given prayer time, but we must remember that the effort to pray is prayer! It is directing the mind and heart to God.

Another way to overcome distractions is to turn them into prayer. For example, if we are worried about a sick friend, we should pray for that friend. If we are concerned about issues of family life or work, we may pray about them.

Distractions sometimes come from fatigue. If you find it hard to stay awake while praying, try changing positions. Walk and pray for a while if this is possible. A breath of fresh air and a cup of coffee or tea can be helpful, especially early in the morning.

It is good to recall that whether we pray at home or church, we pray as members of the body of Christ. Jesus is right there beside us, assisting us and making up for our deficiencies by the power of his prayer. When distracted, let's ask him, as did the apostles, "Lord, teach us to pray." He surely will.

TEMPTATIONS AND SHAMEFUL THOUGHTS

Distractions are especially troubling when they involve temptations or shameful thoughts. A gentleman wrote: "I am trying to grow in my faith. I pray, go to church, and go to confession. But my thoughts are my worst enemy. Sometimes they turn to lust and anger. When I recognize what I am thinking, I pray to Jesus and Mary. I'm scared that I will never be good enough for Jesus."

Bad thoughts, hateful or lustful ideas and images, cross the minds of most people, sometimes at prayer. But unless we want them or deliberately keep them in our consciousness, they are not sins, but temptations, quite likely from Satan, who does not want us to pray. What really matters is not the mere presence of these thoughts, but what we do about them.

The thought of murdering a neighbor might enter our mind when the neighbor's dog barks all night. But as long as we don't deliberately foster hateful ideas, or go out and buy a gun to shoot the neighbor, the thought is not sinful. The temptation to commit some lustful act might come into our head, even during prayer. But if we resist the temptation, we have not sinned. Rather, we have performed a virtuous act.

When angry and lustful thoughts enter our consciousness, we should say a prayer and turn our mind to something else. Such thoughts or temptations become sins only when we deliberately encourage them or when we make plans to sin. What counts is what we do after the thought or temptation crosses our mind.

A good question to ask ourselves when trying to decide if bad thoughts are sinful is: "Do I deliberately try to make them better?" In other words, do I deliberately focus on the thoughts and try to obtain pleasure from them? If so, they are sinful. Otherwise, they are not.

Another way of evaluating whether or not hateful and lustful thoughts are sinful is to examine whether we deliberately do anything to fill our minds with them. A person who reads hate literature or keeps a collection of pornographic pictures is deliberately causing bad thoughts. That person is therefore responsible for the thoughts, and has an obligation to get rid of the pornography and bad literature. On the other hand, people who have turned away from pornography might be troubled by memories of things they have read or seen in the past. But if they have stopped using pornography and are sincerely trying to get rid of the thoughts, they are committing no sin.

When dealing with bad thoughts, we should put our trust in Jesus and try to focus on what is good and peaceful. But we ought to do so without excessive anxiety or worry. If we are too anxious, we can actually trigger the very thoughts we are trying to avoid. For example, we probably don't often think about pink elephants. But if we were promised a million dollars if we didn't think about pink elephants for ten minutes, we probably couldn't think about anything else! So instead of panicking when temptations or bad thoughts come, we should relax, put our trust in Jesus, and peacefully turn our attention to something else.

That something else might very well be Scripture. We might memorize all or part of the following passage, then peacefully reflect on it when troubled by temptation: "...whatever is true, whatever is honorable, whatever is just, whatever is pure, whatever is pleasing, whatever is commendable, if there is any excellence and if there is anything worthy of praise, think about these things" (Philippians 4:8).

REASONS FOR PRAYING, "THY WILL BE DONE"

The following question and comments have been proposed many times in classes and discussions about prayer. Perhaps they have crossed your mind. "Why do we ask for what we want when we are supposed to pray that God's will be done? I can never understand the point of praying to God for something when God knows what we want. Besides, it's not supposed to matter what we want. We should just accept what God knows is best for us."

There are many ways we can pray, "Thy will be done," and many reasons to use these words taught by Jesus in the Lord's Prayer.

First, we live in a world where God's will is often ignored. Every time a sin is committed, God's will is rejected. So we pray, "Thy will be done," that we may be faithful to God's will and that people who disobey God might have a conversion of heart.

Second, we can find ourselves in circumstances where we know what God's will is, but lack the strength to do it. For example, Jesus tells us to forgive enemies. We might be unable to do this on our own. "Thy will be done" is a plea for the grace and strength to do God's will.

Third, we might be in a situation where we don't know what is best. A teacher, for example, has a student who is causing problems. The teacher doesn't know whether to discipline the child firmly, lecture the child, consult with parents, or what. "Thy will be done" asks God for the grace to make the right choice. This is especially important when God's will might involve pain and suffering. Thus Jesus, in the Garden of Gethsemane, prayed: "Father, if it is possible, let this cup pass, yet not my will, but yours be done."

Fourth, we might be sure that what we want is best, but God may know better. Dr. Larry Dossey, as noted in Chapter Four, cites research showing that prayer affects the healing process positively. But research and experience indicate that we can pray for a sick person, and that person might get no better, or even die. Dr. Dossey says that as a physician he would love to have a prayer that always worked. But if all prayers for healing were answered the way we want, no one would ever die or go to heaven. Dr. Dossey uses this example to show that we don't understand all the consequences of prayer. This is why our prayer should always include, "Thy will be done."

Fifth, we might suppose that since God knows what's best for us, there is no reason to pray. However, God does not force blessings or gifts on anyone, and many of God's gifts are conditioned on our asking for them. If we don't recognize where blessings originate, we will lose an important point of contact with God.

So God wants us to ask for the things we need. Prayer turns us to God as the giver of all good things. Jesus says that God already knows what we need before we ask (Matthew 6:8), then proceeds to teach us the Lord's Prayer!

THE LORD'S PRAYER

I've often been asked to explain the meaning of the various phrases of the Lord's Prayer. Expressions such as "Hallowed be thy name" and "Lead us not into temptation" are especially difficult for many believers. A phrase-by-phrase explanation may be helpful.

Our Father. God is addressed as a Father who gave us life so that we might be happy forever in God's presence. We are God's beloved children, and God sees the image of Jesus in us when we pray in his words. We pray, not as individuals, but as members of God's family, joined to brothers and sisters throughout the world who pray in these same words.

Who art in heaven. Heaven is where God is, everywhere. We should say these words with awe as we reflect on the vastness and magnificence of the created universe. The more we learn about the wonders uncovered by astronomers and other scientists, the more we should feel privileged to speak to the Maker of the heavens.

Hallowed be thy name. This means, "May God's name be honored as holy." Fans at a sporting event chant the name of a favorite player. They show appreciation for the athlete's talents and share in his accomplishments by their applause. When we pray the Lord's Prayer, we join the applause of those in heaven and on earth.

Thy kingdom come. We pray that people on earth may accept God's rule and priorities. We pray that God's plan to gather all human beings into the kingdom of heaven may be realized, and that we may humbly submit to God's rule.

Thy will be done on earth as it is in heaven. Jesus did not just teach us to say these words. He said them in the face of his passion and death. What God wants is best. Even in a world where people can do what God doesn't want, God can bring good from evil, light from darkness, resurrection from every cross. God fits all human choices, good and bad, into a plan designed to give eternal joy to all who rely on providence. So we pray that we may follow God's will as do those in heaven. We trust God's will to bring peace and joy to us, as it has to the angels and saints.

Give us this day our daily bread. God knows our bodily needs. We entrust the fulfillment of these needs to God. Our daily bread includes also the spiritual blessings for which we hunger, especially the Eucharist, the Bread that is Christ.

And forgive us our trespasses, as we forgive those who trespass against us. We acknowledge our sins and failings. We recognize that we can receive God's forgiveness only if we forgive others. In forgiving others, we allow God to grant us the gifts of pardon and peace.

And lead us not into temptation. This traditional English translation seems to imply that God could lead us into temptation and thus into sin. But God does not tempt us to sin. A more accurate wording might be, "Do not let us surrender to temptation." We ask God to save us from sin that falsely promises happiness but brings only misery.

But deliver us from evil. Evil and misery entered our world through the tempting of the evil one, Satan. We ask God for the strength and wisdom needed to conquer Satan's lies and to live in the realm of God's grace and peace.

"FOR THINE IS THE KINGDOM..."

In discussions of the Lord's prayer in RCIA classes, the question is invariably asked, "When Catholics pray the Lord's Prayer, why do they omit the words, "For thine is the kingdom, and the power, and the glory, forever and ever"? These words were not in the prayer Jesus taught to his apostles (Matthew 6:9–13) as recorded in the original Greek New Testament. But they were added to the Lord's Prayer in the old *King James Version* long used by English-speaking Protestants. Modern Protestant translations of the Bible, such as the *New Revised Standard Version* or the *Good News for Modern Man,* no longer include these words. Where did the words come from? Most scholars believe that they were added by mistake from an early Christian prayer found in the *Didache* (an early Christian document). The *King James* translators used a source that had the extra words, so they included them in their version of the Bible. (This information may be found in the Protestant resource, *The Interpreter's Bible,* volume 7, pages 314–315). The words, "For the kingdom, the power, and the glory are yours, now and forever," are said by Catholics at Mass, but as a response to the "Deliver us" prayer, as was the custom in the early Church.

THE SAINTS: HAPPY TO HELP US

I received the following note some years ago, but the issue raised about the happiness of the saints in heaven has been mentioned many times. "My father died when I was a little girl. I am not Catholic, but for several years after his death I used to talk to him through prayers. As I got older, I quit doing it, since it didn't square well with my religious beliefs. Since then I have studied the Catholic doctrine that we can pray to loved ones in heaven, and this is truly a comfort. But it raises a question: If a departed loved one realizes that a relative on earth is unhappy or in trouble, wouldn't that cause the departed soul to be unhappy? Doesn't that contradict the idea of heaven as a place without sorrow?"

This note is a beautiful illustration of what Jesus meant in his prayer, "I thank you, Father, Lord of heaven and earth, because you have hidden these things from the wise and the intelligent and have revealed them to infants" (Matthew 11:25). When a little girl prayed to her father, she was responding to an inspiration Jesus placed in her heart, an inspiration in keeping with the doctrine of the Catholic Church. The Church teaches that the saints in heaven are aware of us, that we may speak to them in prayer, that they hear us and help us by their prayers.

As we saw in Chapter Seven, the Bible shows that we have communion with the saints. Jesus is the Vine, and we are joined to him as branches (John 15:1–6), on earth, in purgatory, and in heaven. Scripture reveals that the saints in heaven know what happens here on earth. The Letter to the Hebrews compares life to a race and portrays the saints, victors from the past, as witnesses of our efforts. They are "in the stands" cheering us on. "Therefore, since we are surrounded by so great a cloud of witnesses, let us... run with perseverance the race that is set before us, looking to Jesus the pioneer and perfecter of our faith" (12:1–2).

But what about the concern that those in heaven would be unhappy if they knew what was happening here on earth? One answer comes immediately to mind. If merely being aware of our problems would take away the happiness of those in heaven, Jesus couldn't be happy, and neither could our guardian angels. So knowledge of what happens on earth can coexist with happiness in the residents of heaven.

The saints lived on earth. They know that life here is not a picnic. They know we need all the help we can get. We should not suppose that God might say to them, "Now forget about your children, family, and friends on earth. Their lives are full of problems, so I'm going to put a screen between heaven and earth, and you can pretend that nothing is going wrong." Impossible!

True happiness comes from helping others, not from ignoring their needs. Those who have died and are with Christ want to help us. They can help us by their prayers, for the Bible teaches that we should pray for one another. If our prayers on earth help others, how much more valuable must be the prayers of those in heaven. We can be sure that the saints find joy in being able to assist us and guide us to our true goal in heaven.

Those in heaven have an incredible insight into what life is all about. They know that our sufferings here on earth, when united to those of Christ, can do much good for the Church (Colossians 1:24). They realize that sufferings borne patiently can help bring us to eternal life. They understand what Saint Paul meant when he said, "I consider that the sufferings of this present time are not worth comparing with the glory about to be revealed to us" (Romans 8:18). They see God face to face and are filled with the love and joy of God. They long for us to join them in the happiness of heaven. They want to share with us their insights about trials and sufferings and give us a helping hand.

Every year on November 1 the Church celebrates the Feast of All Saints, reminding us that we can pray not just to those officially canonized by the Church, but to all our loved ones in heaven. So we should pray to our saints in heaven. They enjoy helping us on earth and one day will welcome us to the happiness of heaven.

REPETITION IN PRAYER

Over the years, I've received many letters from Catholics who have been criticized by others because we offer prayers that involve repetition. We are told that Jesus forbade the repetition of prayers, and so we should not pray the rosary or recite litanies.

Those who do not understand our practice of repeating prayers quote the words of Jesus: "When you are praying, do not heap up empty phrases as the Gentiles do; for they think that they will be heard because of their many words" (Matthew 6:7). Does this mean we should not repeat prayers?

Not really. Jesus tells us not to "heap up empty phrases as do the Gentiles," who were pagans. Pagan prayer is not just praying the same prayer often. Pagan prayer is praying to gods that do not exist. Pagan prayer is supposing that God owes us something for each word we utter. Pagan prayer is bargaining with God. Jesus does not forbid us to repeat prayers.

The Bible itself contains prayers with many repetitions. Psalm 136 repeats the phrase "for his steadfast love endures forever" twenty-six times in a litanylike refrain. Psalm 150 repeats the command to "praise" God thirteen times in six verses! Jesus himself repeated prayers, most notably in the Garden of Gethsemane. In Matthew 26:39, 42, and 44, we read that Jesus prayed, "saying the same words" three times: "My Father, if it is possible, let this cup pass from me; yet not what I want but what you want."

When we pray the words of the rosary, we do not "heap up empty phrases as do the Gentiles." We are calming our bodies and focusing our minds so that we can meditate on the mysteries of our faith. The rosary is a great Christian prayer precisely because it helps us to meditate on the saving truths of Christ's life, death, and resurrection.

The prayers we repeat in the rosary are recited according to the mind of Jesus and the words of Scripture. The Our Father, of course, is Jesus' own prayer. It is interesting to note that immediately after Jesus says we are not to "heap up empty phrases as the Gentiles do," he teaches us the Our Father (Matthew 6:9–13). Surely, he expected us to repeat this prayer.

Further, the first part of the Hail Mary is taken from Scripture, the words of the angel Gabriel and of Elizabeth in the first chapter of Luke's Gospel. These words honor Jesus: "Blessed is the fruit of thy womb, Jesus." The second part of the Hail Mary proclaims our belief that Jesus is truly God: "Holy Mary, Mother of God." It honors Mary as one who prays for us to God: "Pray for us sinners now and at the hour of our death." In so many ways, then, as was pointed out in Chapter Seven, the rosary is the Bible translated into prayer.

THE SAINTS AND US

Even the saints had difficulties in prayer, but they could laugh about them as did Padre Pio. There is a story about Saint Teresa of Ávila that shows how saints could handle difficulties with a sense of humor. While riding across a cold mountain stream, she was dumped unceremoniously into the icy water. "If this is the way you treat your friends," she said to the Lord, "it's no wonder you have so few of them!"

Following the lead of the saints, we are not dismayed by problems as we pray. Instead, we turn to Jesus as our teacher in the ways of prayer. We rely on the assistance of the Holy Spirit, for "the Spirit helps us in our weakness...[when] we do not know how to pray as we ought" (Romans 8:26).

QUESTIONS FOR DISCUSSION AND REFLECTION

What are the most significant difficulties you have had in prayer? What are your most important questions about prayer? Where do you find solutions to the difficulties and answers to the questions?

ACTIVITIES

If you have any difficulties with prayer or questions you would like to ask the author, you may contact me at frlukecm@cs.com.

Chapter Nine

HEAVEN: LIVING IN GOD'S PRESENCE FOREVER

⚓

F ather Mike was preaching a parish mission in a small town.
The pastor used the opportunity to take a week's vacation.
So when a prominent citizen died on Monday, Father Mike celebrated the funeral Mass two days later. The church was packed
with family and friends, and children from the parish school
formed the choir. As Father Mike entered the sanctuary to begin
the funeral rites, he noticed that the paschal candle had not been
placed before the altar. He asked a server to get it while he and
the other servers went to the church entrance to receive the body.
What Father Mike didn't know was that the school children,
before the funeral was scheduled, had planned a Mass for that
day. They had decorated the paschal candle with the theme of
the school Mass. As Father Mike walked back to the altar, he
saw the paschal candle emblazoned with a huge banner bearing
the words, "Bloom Where You Are Planted." Says Father Mike,
"I hope the family has forgiven me."

Well, the words would have been more appropriate as the
theme for a school Mass, but there was meaning for a funeral.
When a person's body is buried in the grave, the story of that
person's life is only beginning. Saint Paul wrote concerning the
resurrection of the body, "What you sow does not come to life
unless it dies....So it is with the resurrection of the dead. What is
sown is perishable, what is raised is imperishable....It is sown a

148

physical body, it is raised a spiritual body" (1 Corinthians 15:36, 42–44). We do bloom where we are planted!

DEATH AS BIRTH

When a seed is sown and a plant springs forth from the soil, death becomes life. But Jesus teaches us an even more important truth: Death is birth. After Jesus died on the cross, his body was taken down and placed in a tomb. His body was separated from his human soul, but both soul and body remained united to his divine person. Saved from corruption, he appeared on Easter Sunday, risen and glorious.

Jesus, of course, did not slumber in the grave until his body rose. As the Apostles' Creed proclaims, Jesus "descended into hell." Here the word *hell* does not signify the place of eternal punishment. Rather, it is an ancient usage denoting the abode of the dead. The Creed means that Jesus really died, that he appeared to the holy souls who had gone before him and were awaiting final redemption. In the traditional phrase, he "opened the gates of heaven."

Jesus appeared in spirit to all those who had died, as Saint Peter explains. "For Christ also suffered for sins once for all, the righteous for the unrighteous, in order to bring you to God. He was put to death in the flesh, but made alive in the spirit, in which also he went and made a proclamation to the spirits in prison" (1 Peter 3:18–19).

Death did not limit Jesus. It was birth to new life that expanded his horizons as a human being and allowed him to minister even to those who had died (see CCC 624–637).

FREED FROM FEAR OF DEATH

Jesus turned death into birth for all who follow him. He invites us to trust that he will bring us through death to new life. Jesus accepted the cross "so that through death he might...free those who all their lives were held in slavery by the fear of death" (Hebrews 2:14–15). We have every reason to believe him. After all, we have already died once, and death turned out to be birth.

We spent nine months in our mother's womb. Then we outgrew that environment. The system that kept us alive could no longer sustain us. We died to life in the womb, but death turned out to be birth. We moved from darkness to light. Not confined to the womb, we were held in the loving arms of parents who embraced us and welcomed us to new life. We found ourselves in a much larger world where there were opportunities for growth, knowledge, and love that surpassed anything in the womb.

This life too has limits. Our bodies will wear out because of age, illness, or accident, and we will die. But once again darkness will turn to light. We will move from the narrow confines of earth into the embrace of One who loves us. We will find ourselves face to face with Jesus, fully alive in a new world with opportunities for growth, knowledge, and love that go beyond anything on earth.

Scripture invites us to reflect on this new life. "See, the home of God is among mortals. / He will dwell with them as their God; / they will be his peoples, / and God himself will be with them; / he will wipe every tear from their eyes. Death will be no more; mourning and crying and pain will be no more, / for the first things have passed away" (Revelation 21:3–4).

PRAYER AS A PATH TO HEAVEN

Heaven, then, is living in God's presence. The life of prayer, as we saw in Chapter One, is the habit of being in the presence of God, so there is a close connection between prayer and heaven. Prayer is an important pathway to heaven.

God gives us life here on earth so that we may be equipped for heaven. God is perfect knowledge and love. We must open mind, heart, and soul to the beauty, truth, and love God offers through Jesus. Prayer helps us do just that, to "get in shape" for heaven.

Those who are not properly prepared for a hike on beautiful mountain terrain won't be able to enjoy the scenery. Those who raft down the Grand Canyon without training or preparation will not fully appreciate the thrills in store for them. We need prayer to prepare ourselves for the breathtaking beauty and ecstasy of heaven.

At prayer we communicate with God our Father, who gave us life. We speak with Jesus, who by his death, resurrection, and ascension shows us the way to eternal happiness. We are united to the Holy Spirit, who helps us understand why we are here and where we are going. In prayer, God fine-tunes our abilities for our eternal destiny.

PRAYER AND THE PROMISE OF ETERNAL LIFE

We may have moments of doubt about the reality of eternal life. Satan certainly wants us to think there is no heaven, and plants seeds of doubt whenever possible. Meditation on our eternal destiny as proclaimed in Scripture can give assurance that our faith is not in vain.

Heaven is referred to in Old Testament books like Wisdom, which mentions the "prize for blameless souls" (2:22). Jesus leaves no doubt about the reality of eternal life: "This is indeed the will of my Father, that all who see the Son and believe in him may have eternal life; and I will raise them up on the last day" (John 6:40). This was no vague promise of some kind of reincarnation or new-age absorption into the infinite. Jesus said to the criminal who was crucified with him, "[T]oday you will be with me in Paradise" (Luke 23:43). Just as the person who dies to life in the womb is the one born into this world, so the person who dies to this life is the one who enters eternal life. Meditation on Paul's great testimony to the certainty of our own resurrection (1 Corinthians 15) should also be an important part of our prayer and preparation for heaven.

The Church teaches we will be judged at the moment of death, and calls this event the *particular judgment* (CCC 1021–1022). Scripture says that "it is appointed for mortals to die once, and after that the judgment" (Hebrews 9:27). We will stand in the presence of God and see our life on earth as God does. We will clearly grasp the evil of sin and the incredible love of God. At that moment our eternal destiny, whether heaven or hell, will be decided. Some will enter the joy of heaven. Some the temporary state of purification called purgatory. And some, tragically, the awful pain of never-ending hell.

But the total meaning of our lives will not be complete until the world ends. Someone's words and example might bring another to Christ. That person may in turn help others, resulting in good deeds that continue through the ages. An evil life, on the other hand, can have repercussions that last for centuries. So, at the end of time Jesus will bring human history to a close in a final judgment that will not change the results of the particular judgment, but will bring the full consequences of our deeds to light.

The Bible and Church have given such names to the end of the world as the End Time, *Parousia*, General Judgment, Last Judgment, Day of the Lord, and Second Coming of Christ. In describing these events, the Bible speaks vividly of angels, trumpets, fire, falling stars, and people being caught up in the air (Matthew 24:29–31; 25:31–46; Mark 13:24–27; 1 Thessalonians 4:16–17; Revelation 20:11–15). These terms are poetic and should not be taken as literal descriptions of how the world will end.

The Church has not made a dogmatic statement on the exact meaning of such passages. Artists paint pictures of bodies rising from graves in response to angelic trumpets, but the essential meaning of the resurrection of the body may be that our risen bodies will have a new relationship to the universe. Our spiritual bodies will in some way be glorified. For "...our citizenship is in heaven, and it is from there that we are expecting a Savior, the Lord Jesus Christ. He will transform the body of our humiliation that it may be conformed to the body of his glory, by the power that also enables him to make all things subject to himself" (Philippians 3:20–21).

Before the last day, all things on Earth are moving toward completion. After the last day, God's masterpiece of creation will be seen in all its glory, and the elect will be active participants in it. Heaven will be glorious before the end of time, and, somehow, even more glorious when time ceases. How this will occur is beyond our ability to imagine. But we can meditate and pray about it, and grow in our assurance that God, with divine wisdom and power, will transform the universe into "new heavens and a new earth" (2 Peter 3:13; see also *CCC* 1023–1065).

PRAYER AS A TASTE OF ETERNAL LIFE

Some people imagine that heaven must be rather dull, perhaps floating around on clouds and strumming harps. Nothing could be further from the truth. "'What no eye has seen, nor ear heard, / nor the human heart conceived, / what God has prepared for those who love him'—these things God has revealed to us through the Spirit" (1 Corinthians 2:9–10). Some of our time at prayer should be devoted to considering what God has prepared and revealed to us through the Spirit. This can give us a proper longing for heaven, a realization that heaven is worth any sacrifice.

Jesus could even long for his passion and death because they would bring him to the glory of heaven. On the night before he died, he prayed, "So now, Father, glorify me in your own presence with the glory that I had in your presence before the world existed" (John 17:5). Not long afterward, Paul would say, "I consider that the sufferings of this present time are not worth comparing with the glory about to be revealed to us" (Romans 8:18).

Jesus teaches that heaven is so wonderful that everything on earth is insignificant when measured against heaven. "For what will it profit them if they gain the whole world but forfeit their life?" (Matthew 16:26).

What will heaven be like? We might begin with verses 3 and 4 of the twenty-first chapter of Revelation. Heaven is being in the embrace of God forever. It is freedom from sorrow, suffering, and death. It is the realization of perfect peace and security.

The greatest joy of heaven will be to see God. "Blessed are the pure of heart," promises Jesus, "for they will see God" (Matthew 5:8). Catholic tradition calls this the *beatific vision* because of the happiness it will bring us. And what an incredible experience it will be to stand in the presence of our Creator, to realize that what we have been longing for is now ours forever, to feel completely loved and to love without limits.

To appreciate this, we might visualize great moments of joy—parents holding their child for the first time, holidays with family, the company of dear friends, a safe landing after a perilous flight, word from physicians that we are cured. If we put all these moments together, then we can begin to imagine the happiness that will be ours when we arrive at our true home in heaven and stand in the presence of God.

Prayer sometimes offers a taste of heaven in more dramatic fashion. Some of the saints have had moments of ecstasy at prayer that could only be described as "a little bit of heaven." Saint Paul says that he was "caught up to the third heaven—whether in the body or out of the body I do not know; God knows...caught up into Paradise and heard things that are not to be told, that no mortal is permitted to repeat" (2 Corinthians 12:2–4).

Saint Teresa of Ávila and Padre Pio experienced times of trial at prayer, but they also enjoyed moments of ecstasy. I've talked to friends who had the privilege of witnessing Pope John Paul II at prayer and seeing an "aura" around him. "We knew God was there," they said. Not everyone has such moments of ecstasy at prayer. But those of us who haven't are still blessed to know those moments are real and foreshadow the bliss of all who die in Christ. "Blessed are the dead who from now on die in the Lord" (Revelation 14:13).

EXCITEMENT IN HEAVEN

There is another dimension of heaven that should be considered—excitement. If you've ever had the privilege of meeting a famous person, you were probably excited about the prospect. Imagine the excitement of meeting Jesus Christ! Of seeing God face to face! "Beloved, we are God's children now; what we will be has not yet been revealed. What we do know is this: when he is revealed, we will be like him, for we will see him as he is" (1 John 3:2).

Imagine too the joy of making the acquaintance of Mary and Joseph, of your patron saints, of your guardian angel. Imagine the happiness you'll feel when you meet relatives, those you knew on earth, and those you'd only heard about when their exploits were told you as a child.

Or imagine the excitement experienced by sports fans whose teams have won the World Series or the Super Bowl. Picture the exultation felt by racing fans when their favorite driver wins the Indy 500 or the NASCAR championship. On entering heaven, we will experience far greater joy and exultation, as what Saint

Paul wrote becomes clear: "Death [is] swallowed up in victory" (1 Corinthians 15:54). Earthly victories have their limits. The St. Louis Rams, my favorite football team, won Super Bowl XXXIV, and that brought joy to St. Louis. They haven't won another championship, and each successive season lessens the impact of the big win. But the victory of life over death that Saint Paul speaks of will last forever. It will be so decisive and so complete that we'll need all eternity to savor it.

Then there is the excitement of those who enjoy stage performances, musicals, operas, and other entertainment. Some members of the audience are almost breathless with anticipation before a great show begins. When an exceptional performance ends and the entire audience rises to applaud and call for an encore, the excitement and joy seem almost to explode. But no performance on earth can be compared with the perfection and glory that will be evident when God's design for our salvation is on stage for all humanity to see and enjoy. There will also be the heavenly choirs of angels and saints (Revelation 15:2–4), putting any earthly performance to shame. The *Catechism of the Catholic Church* describes this great chorus of song and worship as a gathering of the angels and saints, led by Mary, and including "a great multitude that no one could count, from every nation, from all tribes and peoples and languages" (Revelation 7:9; CCC 1138).

Consider also the happiness we enjoy while sightseeing. Vacations to places like the Grand Canyon, Yellowstone, or the Great Smoky Mountains bring fun and excitement to millions every year. But such vacations have limits. There's traffic that slows progress to a crawl, the cost of travel, and the fact that vacations seem to end too soon. But heaven will bring possibilities for scenery we can only imagine here on earth. The entire universe will be on our map. We will have spiritual bodies unlimited by space or time. We will be able to enjoy any corner of creation in the company of friends, of relatives who lived generations before or after us, of saints and angels. There will be no lost luggage, no need to seek out accommodations. The vacation will never end. It's enough to make you say, "I can hardly wait!"

Praying for Heaven

Prayerful consideration of life after death can help us trust in Christ's promise of eternal joy. Nevertheless, there will be moments when death seems fearful. We must remember that God does not give us the grace to die until it is time to die. But we can and should pray now for a happy death.

We are blessed as Catholics to have many wonderful resources for such prayer. First, there is the Bible, with its many teachings on life after death. Consider, for example, Paul's reflection on Jesus as the One who leads us through death to eternal joy:

> I want to know Christ and the power of his resurrection and the sharing of his sufferings by becoming like him in his death, if somehow I may attain the resurrection from the dead.
>
> Not that I have already obtained this or have already reached the goal; but I press on to make it my own, because Christ Jesus has made me his own. Beloved, I do not consider that I have made it my own; but this one thing I do: forgetting what lies behind and straining forward to what lies ahead, I press on toward the goal for the prize of the heavenly call of God in Christ Jesus (Philippians 3:10–14).

We have the *Catechism of the Catholic Church*, which presents the Church's doctrine on death and life after death (1020–1060). Meditation on the Bible and *Catechism* can encourage us to pray for a happy death and to trust that Jesus will bring us through death to eternal happiness.

The Stations of the Cross show us what Jesus suffered to bring us through death. They tell how Jesus shares our sufferings and will share also with us his victory over death. The rosary, especially in its sorrowful and glorious mysteries, encourages us to consider Christ's death and resurrection as a pledge that Jesus will be with us at the moment of death to bring us to eternal happiness.

The Hail Mary offers assurance of our Blessed Mother's care for us in life and death. We ask Mary, who stood close to her Son as he died on the cross, to be close to us: "Holy Mary, Mother of God, pray for us sinners, now and at the hour of our death."

Another traditional prayer invokes the Holy Family: "Jesus, Mary, and Joseph, I give you my heart and my soul. Jesus, Mary, and Joseph, assist me in my last moments. Jesus, Mary, and Joseph, may I breathe forth my soul in peace with you."

My sister, Joann, often said this prayer with my mother during her last illness. When Joann visited Mom on the Sunday after Christmas, Mom said, "They're coming." Joann wasn't sure what these words meant, but their meaning became apparent when Mom died gently that afternoon. She had often asked for the grace to breathe forth her soul in peace with Jesus, Mary, and Joseph. On the morning of her death, I'm sure she saw them coming to assist her in her last moments. She died in their arms, for the Sunday after Christmas is the Feast of the Holy Family.

WHEN DEATH COMES

Jesus was with Saint Joseph when he died, and Jesus is with believers today through the sacraments as death draws near. In the sacrament of penance, Jesus forgives our sins. Through the anointing of the sick, Christ comes to the afflicted to raise them up (James 5:14–15). This always means spiritual healing. It may mean physical healing. And it means complete healing when Jesus raises us from death to eternal life. Not long before my mother died, she became weak with pneumonia. I went to her hospital room and said, "Mom, I'm going to anoint you and give you holy Communion." She smiled and whispered, "Good. Then I'll be all ready to fly away to heaven." Through the anointing, Christ does take the sick by the hand and raise them up to eternal life. Through holy Communion, Jesus unites us to himself as a foretaste of our heavenly union with him: "Whoever eats of this bread will live forever" (John 6:51).

"FATHER, INTO YOUR HANDS I COMMEND MY SPIRIT"

Justin Cardinal Rigali, in his book, *Show Us Your Mercy and Love,* describes another aspect of prayer that will prepare us for death: We can imitate Jesus in laying down our life freely. On the cross, Jesus surrendered his life to the Father with the words, "Father, into your hands I commend my spirit" (Luke 23:46). Because Jesus laid down his life for us, we have the power to lay down our life. In prayer, we can anticipate the moment of our death and offer it to the Father in union with the death of Jesus. Cardinal Rigali explains:

> The Father wills that we pass through death—redeemed death— the death that is now linked not only with sin but also with the death of Jesus and his resurrection.... Seen in this perspective, death is the moment to give all, to surrender all with Jesus and in union with his sacrifice. All of this can be anticipated by an act of our will, by an act of our love. When anticipated by an act of loving acceptance, death is an opportunity to say yes to the Father, just as Jesus did (p. 75).

Death is our final opportunity to give everything to God, to make up for any sin we've ever committed. In prayer, we can anticipate this total gift of ourselves and so find joy and peace each time we say, "Father, into your hands I commend my spirit." No longer victims of a death that seems beyond our control, we freely take control of our death. Like Jesus, with Jesus, we can say, "No one takes it from me, but I lay it down of my own accord. I have power to lay it down" (John 10:18).

Every night can be a peaceful rehearsal for death. We lie down to rest, trusting that we will rise again in the morning. As we retire, we can offer the prayer to Jesus the Healer suggested in Chapter Five. Then we can peacefully anticipate the moment of death, saying with Jesus, "Father, into your hands I commend my spirit." We do so with the certainty that when the sleep of death finally comes, it will be an awakening to new life.

PRAYER AT ITS BEST

All this is beautifully expressed in John Cardinal Newman's prayer for a happy death:

> Oh, my Lord and Savior, support me in that hour in the strong arms of Thy sacraments, and by the fresh fragrance of Thy consolations. Let the absolving words be said over me, and the holy oil sign and seal me, and Thy own Body be my food, and Thy Blood my sprinkling; and let my sweet Mother Mary breathe on me, and my angel whisper peace to me, and my glorious saints...smile upon me; that in them all, and through them all, I may receive the gift of perseverance, and die, as I desire to live, in Thy faith, in Thy Church, in Thy service, and in Thy love. Amen. (www.newmanreader.org/works/meditations/meditations8.html#death)

As we anticipate death with hope, peace, and joy, Jesus will be with us each time we pray. And he will be with us at the moment of death. Lisa, a former student of mine, sent a note telling about the death of her mother:

My Mom was diagnosed with ovarian cancer several years ago. She was in the hospital during her last days, and the family gathered in her room as she received the last rites. The next day she and I were alone. All was quiet, as she hadn't spoken in a week or so. Suddenly, she said aloud, "Jesus, Jesus is here!" I told her to reach out and take his hand. She passed away the next day. I miss her so much, but knowing that Jesus was with her when she was dying has brought peace.

What Lisa's mother experienced at death, the presence of Jesus, begins with the life of prayer. "[T]he life of prayer is the habit of being in the presence of...God and in communion with him" (CCC 2565). When we pray as Jesus taught us, we enter God's presence here on earth. Ultimately, a life of prayer will lead us to God's presence in heaven, and the joy heaven will bring.

This is not wishful thinking. It is Christ's promise: "In my Father's house there are many dwelling places. If it were not so, would I have told you that I go to prepare a place for you? And if I go and prepare a place for you, I will come again and will take you to myself, so that where I am, there you may be also" (John 14:2–3). "I will see you again, and your hearts will rejoice, and no one will take your joy from you" (John 16:22).

Heaven is living in God's presence forever. It will be prayer at its best!

QUESTIONS FOR
DISCUSSION AND REFLECTION

Have you ever read 1 Corinthians 15 in its entirety? What does it say to you about the reality of the resurrection of the body? Are there other passages in Scripture that have strengthened your belief in the reality of eternal life? Have you ever thought of death as birth? Does thinking about your own death frighten you? What are some ways you can lessen any fear you might have about death? Does heaven seem exciting to you? What is there about heaven that you look forward to most? What is your favorite prayer for a happy death?

ACTIVITIES

Take a few moments to relax in silence and peace. Then imagine what it will be like to enter heaven. The beauty is breathtaking. Jesus stands there with arms open to embrace you. You see members of your family and your closest friends walking toward you. The last time you saw them, they were worn with age and illness. Now they are so vibrantly alive that you are overwhelmed. You embrace and talk and laugh. Suddenly, the realization fills your whole being: "We'll never again be parted. There is nothing to fear, nothing to be anxious about. No more sadness, no more hatred, no more sickness, no more tears, no more death. This is what I've always wanted; this is what I was made for."

As you pray, consider that heaven is your true home. Ask Jesus to help you keep this always in mind. Talk to your favorite saints and to friends and family who have died. Ask them to stay close to you and help you live in such a way that one day you will join them in heaven.

POPULAR CATHOLIC PRAYERS

MORNING OFFERING

Most holy and adorable Trinity, one God in three Persons, I praise you and give you thanks for all the favors you have bestowed on me. Your goodness has preserved me until now. I offer you my whole being and in particular all my thoughts, words, and deeds, together with all the trials I may undergo this day. Give them your blessing. May your divine love animate them and may they serve your greater glory.

I make this morning offering in union with the divine intentions of Jesus Christ who offers himself daily in the holy sacrifice of the Mass, and in union with Mary, his Virgin Mother, and our Mother, who was always the faithful handmaid of the Lord. Amen.

APOSTLES' CREED

I believe in God, the Father almighty, creator of heaven and earth. I believe in Jesus Christ, his only Son, our Lord. He was conceived by the power of the Holy Spirit and born of the Virgin Mary. He suffered under Pontius Pilate, was crucified, died, and was buried. He descended to the dead. On the third day he rose again. He ascended into heaven, and is seated at the right hand of the Father. He will come again to judge the living and the dead. I believe in the Holy Spirit, the holy Catholic Church, the communion of saints, the forgiveness of sins, the resurrection of the body, and the life everlasting. Amen.

HAIL MARY

Hail Mary, full of grace. The Lord is with thee. Blessed art thou among women, and blessed is the fruit of thy womb, Jesus. Holy Mary, Mother of God, pray for us sinners, now and at the hour of our death. Amen.

OUR FATHER

Our Father, who art in heaven, hallowed be thy name; thy kingdom come, thy will be done on earth as it is in heaven. Give us this day our daily bread, and forgive us our trespasses, as we forgive those who trespass against us; and lead us not into temptation, but deliver us from evil. Amen.

DOXOLOGY

Glory be to the Father, and to the Son, and to the Holy Spirit; as it was in the beginning, is now and ever shall be, world without end. Amen.

ACT OF CONTRITION

My God, I am sorry for my sins with all my heart. In choosing to do wrong and failing to do good, I have sinned against you whom I should love above all things. I firmly intend, with your help, to do penance, to sin no more, and to avoid whatever leads me to sin. Our Savior Jesus Christ suffered and died for us. In his name, my God, have mercy. Amen.

ACT OF FAITH

O my God, I firmly believe that you are one God in three divine Persons, Father, Son, and Holy Spirit; I believe that your divine Son became man and died for our sins, and that he will come to judge the living and the dead. I believe these and all the truths which the holy Catholic Church teaches, because you revealed them, who can neither deceive nor be deceived. Amen.

ACT OF HOPE

O my God, relying on your infinite goodness and promises, I hope to obtain pardon for my sins, the help of your grace, and life everlasting, through the merits of Jesus Christ, my Lord and Redeemer. Amen.

ACT OF LOVE

O my God, I love you above all things, with my whole heart and soul, because you are all good and worthy of all my love. I love my neighbor as myself for the love of you. I forgive all who have injured me and I ask pardon of all whom I have injured. Amen.

MEMORARE

Remember, O most gracious Virgin Mary, that never was it known that anyone who fled to your protection, implored your help, or sought your intercession was left unaided. Inspired with this confidence, I fly unto you, O virgin of virgins, my Mother.

To you I come, before you I stand, sinful and sorrowful. O Mother of the Word Incarnate, despise not my petitions, but in your mercy, hear and answer me. Amen.

HAIL HOLY QUEEN

Hail, holy Queen, mother of mercy, our life, our sweetness, and our hope. To you do we cry, poor banished children of Eve; to you do we send up our sighs, mourning and weeping in this valley of tears. Turn then, O most gracious advocate, your eyes of mercy toward us, and after this our exile, show unto us the blessed fruit of your womb, Jesus. O clement, O loving, O sweet Virgin Mary. Pray that we may be made worthy of the promises of Christ.

GRACE BEFORE MEALS

Bless us, O Lord, and these your gifts, which we are about to receive from your bounty, through Christ, our Lord. Amen.

Thanksgiving After Meals

We give thanks for all your benefits, almighty God, who live and reign forever. May the souls of the faithful departed, through the mercy of God, rest in peace. Amen.

Prayer Before a Crucifix

Look down upon me, good and gentle Jesus, while before your face I humbly kneel, and with a burning soul pray and beseech you to fix deep in my heart lively sentiments of faith, hope, and charity, true contrition for my sins, and a firm purpose of amendment, while I contemplate with great love and tender pity your five wounds, pondering over them within me, calling to mind the words that David, your prophet, said of you, my good Jesus, "They have pierced my hands and my feet; they have numbered all my bones."

Prayer to Your Guardian Angel

Angel of God, my guardian dear, to whom God's love commits me here, ever this day be at my side, to light and guard, to rule and guide. Amen.

BIBLIOGRAPHY

Saint Augustine. *Treatise on John*, tract. 84:1–2.

International Committee on English in the Liturgy, National Conference of Catholic Bishops. *Shorter Book of Blessings*. New York: Catholic Book Publishing, 1990.

International Committee on English in the Liturgy, National Conference of Catholic Bishops. *The Liturgy of the Hours*. New York: Catholic Book Publishing, 1975.

Bryson, Bill. *A Short History of Nearly Everything*. New York: Broadway Books, 2003.

Office for the Catechism, United States Catholic Conference. *Catechism of the Catholic Church*, 2nd ed. Washington, DC: USCC Publishing Services, 1997.

Buttrick, George A., ed. *The Interpreter's Bible*, vol. 7. Nashville, TN: Abingdon Press, 1952.

Dossey, Larry. *Healing Words: The Power of Prayer and the Practice of Medicine*. San Francisco: HarperSanFrancisco, 1993.

John Paul II. On the Eucharist in Its Relationship to the Church *(Ecclesia De Eucharistia, 25)*, April 17, 2003.

Komp, Diane M. *Images of Grace*. Grand Rapids, MI: Zondervan Publishing House, 1996.

Lukefahr, Oscar. *A Catholic Guide to the Bible*, revised edition. Liguori, MO: Liguori Publications, 1998.

_____. *Christ's Mother and Ours: A Catholic Guide to Mary*. Liguori, MO: Liguori Publications, 2003.

_____. *The Privilege of Being Catholic*. Liguori, MO: Liguori Publications, 1993.

_____. *The Search for Happiness: Four Levels of Emotional and Spiritual Growth.* Liguori, MO: Liguori Publications, 2002.

_____. *"We Believe...": A Survey of the Catholic Faith,* revised edition. Liguori, MO: Liguori Publications, 1995.

_____. *We Worship: A Guide to the Catholic Mass.* Liguori, MO: Liguori Publications, 2004.

McKibben, Bill. "A Deeper Shade of Green." *National Geographic,* August 2006, 41.

New Revised Standard Version of the Bible: Catholic Edition. Nashville, TN: Catholic Bible Press. 1993.

Rigali, Justin Cardinal. *Show Us Your Mercy and Love.* Mahwah, NJ: Paulist Press, 2003.

Rossetti, Stephen J. *The Joy of Priesthood.* Notre Dame, IN: Ave Maria Press, 2005.

The Sacramentary. New York: Catholic Book Publishing Company, 1985.

Schroeder, Gerald L. *The Science of God.* New York: The Free Press, 1997.

Ward, J. Neville. *Five for Sorrow, Ten for Joy: Meditations on the Rosary,* revised edition. Cambridge, MA: Cowley Publications, 1985.

Wiesel, Elie. *Night,* transl. Marion Wiesel. New York: Hill and Wang, 2006.